THE VIA FRANCIGENA –
CANTERBURY TO ROME

1: Canterbury to the Great St Bernard Pass

About the Author

A chance viewing of a television programme in the early 1970s led to the author's interest in the Pilgrim Road to Santiago, at that time barely known in Britain. A walker most of her life, Alison had the opportunity to walk the 1000-mile *camino* from Le Puy-en-Velay to Santiago all in one go in 1990, a time which coincided, fortuitously, with Cicerone looking for an author to write an original guide in English to the Spanish section of the route. Since then she has walked and explored many of the pilgrim roads through Europe (France, Germany, Switzerland, Portugal), as well as those she has written about.

Alison is a former teacher of French, German and Spanish to adults, and her other interests include playing the French horn.

Other Cicerone guides by the author
The Way of St James – Le Puy to the Pyrenees
The Way of St James – Pyrenees–Santiago–Finisterre
Vía de la Plata – Seville/Granada to Santiago
The Pilgrim Road to Nidaros – Oslo to Trondheim

THE VIA FRANCIGENA –
CANTERBURY TO ROME

1: Canterbury to the Great St Bernard Pass

Alison Raju

CICERONE

2 POLICE SQUARE, MILNTHORPE, CUMBRIA LA7 7PY
www.cicerone.co.uk

© Alison Raju 2011
First edition 2011
ISBN: 978 1 85284 487 5

Printed by KHL Printing, Singapore
A catalogue record for this book is available from the British Library.
Photographs by Michael Krier unless otherwise indicated.

FFRandonnée 🚶 The routes of the GR®, PR® and GRP® paths in this guide
www.ffrandonnee.fr have been reproduced with the permission of the Fédération
Française de la Randonnée Pédestre holder of the exclusive
rights of the routes. The names GR®, PR® and GRP® are registered trademarks.

© FFRP 2011 for all GR®, PR® and GRP® paths appearing in this work

Dedication
For all those who begin their journey as a walker and end it as a pilgrim.

Acknowledgements
I would like to thank Chantal Delannoy (Arras), Catherine Broussard
(Châteauvillain), Michèle Mouneyrac (Besançon) and Marigold Fox for their
very considerable assistance in the preparation of this guide, Eric Walker for the
original artwork on which the route profile on page 12 is based, and Graham
and Ellie Scholes for proofreading all the text.

Advice to Readers

Readers are advised that, while every effort is made by our authors to ensure
the accuracy of guidebooks as they go to print, changes can occur during
the lifetime of an edition. Please check Updates on this book's page on the
Cicerone website (www.cicerone.co.uk) before planning your trip. We would
also advise that you check information about such things as transport, accommodation and shops locally. Even rights of way can be altered over time. We
are always grateful for information about any discrepancies between a guidebook and the facts on the ground, sent by email to info@cicerone.co.uk or
by post to Cicerone, 2 Police Square, Milnthorpe LA7 7PY, United Kingdom.

Front cover: Pilgrim riding into Canterbury: detail from Canterbury Cathedral's
west window (Section 1)

CONTENTS

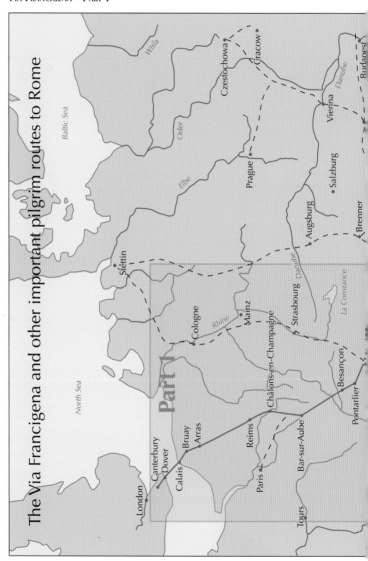

The Via Francigena and other important pilgrim routes to Rome

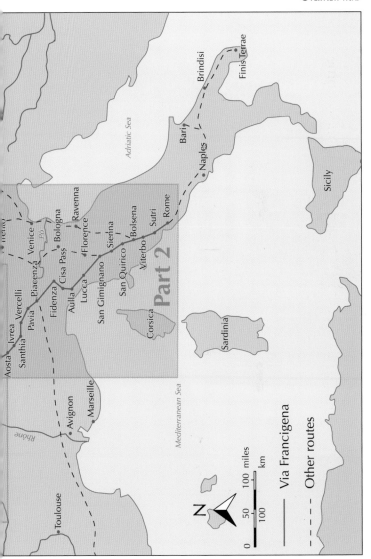

Via Francigena
- - - Other routes

Bridge at Ornans

Map Key

⬛⬛⬛⬛⬛▦	road/tunnel	•	town/village
▬▬▬▬▬▬	walk route on road/alternative	·	habitation
▬ ▬ ▬ ▬	railway	†	cemetery
————— -----	walk route/alternative route	⌂	cathedral
～～～～	river or canal	♦	chapel/church
▬▬▬▬▬▬	ridge	St/Ste	Saint/Sainte

Abbreviations used in route descriptions

L/R	turn/fork left or right
(L)/(R)	to your left or right (feature described in the text)
KSO	keep straight on
KSO(L)/KSO(R)	keep straight on left or right (at a fork)
FB	footbridge
FP	footpath
SCRB	shops, cafés, restaurants, banks
CH	chambre d'hôte
YH	youth hostel
K	kitchen/cooking facilities
resto	restaurant
PO	post office
TO	tourist office
SI	Syndicat d'Initiative (tourist office)
PS	pilgrim stamp
X	closed/except
CD	cash dispenser
HT	high tension (cables)
AIVF	Associazione Internationale della Via Francigena
All facilities	a full range of shops, banks, restaurants, hotels, medical centre and public transport
▼	see footnote below (blue text)

Reims cathedral, exterior (Section 3)

INTRODUCTION

Voie Romaine after Coolus (Section 4)

The Via Francigena ('the way through France') is a long-distance walk with a difference – a pilgrimage on foot from Canterbury to Rome. People have been making pilgrimages to Rome since the fourth century. Early pilgrims from Britain usually went across to what is now Germany and then down the Rhine, but from about the eighth century that began to change. Many of those who started in Canterbury, or passed through it on their way, would have taken much the same route as the one described in this book, through northern and eastern France, Switzerland and over the Great St Bernard Pass into Italy – and from there southwards to the 'Eternal City', a total of some 1900km. This route has become known nowadays as the Via Francigena (pronounced with the emphasis on the 'i' – 'francheegena'), and was made a European Cultural Itinerary by the Council of Europe in 1994 (in the same way that the Camino de Santiago was in 1987).

Many people who undertake pilgrim routes such as the Via Francigena, and that to Santiago de Compostela through north and north-western Spain, are not experienced walkers. They have often never done any serious walking in their lives and many will never do any again. On a pilgrim route, as in the past, walking is a means of transport, a means to an end, rather than an activity for its own sake. And while most long-distance footpaths, in Britain and France, for example, avoid not only large towns but also even quite small villages, the route to Rome, because of its historic origins and the need for shelter, deliberately seeks them out.

Relatively few people make this journey on foot at present, regardless of their starting point, but numbers have begun to increase gradually, and in 2009 some 2500 people walked, cycled or went there on horseback (compared, for example, to the 145,877 who made the pilgrimage to Santiago de Compostela in the same year). However, by no means all of them started in either Canterbury or places in their own countries, and a large number of those who reported their arrival to the authorities in the

Vatican had only done a fairly small section of the route in Italy. To qualify for a Testimonium (certificate of pilgrimage) walkers must have come from at least Acquapendente (100km), and cyclists must have completed the 200km from Lucca.

The modern pilgrim

One of the main differences between modern pilgrims and their historical counterparts, whether they walk, cycle or ride, is that very few return home by the same means of transport. The Via Francigena as an early 21st-century pilgrim route has thus become a 'one-way street', and it is unusual today to encounter anyone with either enough time or the inclination to return by the same means as they used on their outward journey.

People today make the pilgrimage from Canterbury (or other starting points in Europe) to Rome for a

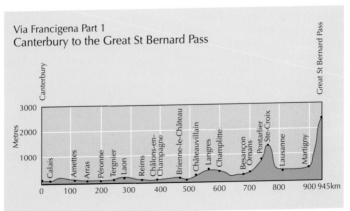

Via Francigena Part 1
Canterbury to the Great St Bernard Pass

variety of reasons. For some it is just another long-distance walk. Many, but by no means all, have already walked or ridden the pilgrim road to Santiago de Compostela (see 'History' and 'A challenging pilgrim route' below) and would like to experience another of the three great Christian pilgrim destinations (the ultimate one being Jerusalem). For others, however, the journey on foot or by bicycle will be their first pilgrim undertaking, and their motives may be historical, cultural, sporting or religious, or some combination of all of these. For many people it may also be a significant action or event in their lives – to mark their retirement, perhaps, to fill the gap between studying and taking a first job, or the opportunity to take time out to decide which way to go next after a turning point in their lives.

Pilgrims in the 21st century are of all ages, from all walks of life and, nowadays, from all parts of the globe, not just from Western Europe. Some travel alone, some in twos and threes, some (in the Italian section in particular) in quite large groups, usually those on foot. Many complete the entire journey in one stretch, and this is recommended wherever possible, as otherwise the journey tends to become just a series of disjointed holidays, where the walker never really 'leaves home', rather than an actual pilgrimage. Others with more limited time have to cover a section at a time over several years.

Most of those who walk the Via Francigena, like those who have already experienced the Camino de Santiago, and especially those who have been able to do the whole route in one go, would probably agree that it has changed their lives in some way, even if they did not set out with this intention.

Hospice du Grand Saint-Bernard seen from the Italian side of the lake (Section 6)

A guide for walkers

A cyclists' guide to the route from Canterbury to Rome is available in English (see bibliography in Appendix A), and there are several walkers' guidebooks (in Italian) to the route through Italy, but this book is, at present, the only dedicated walkers' guide in any language to the whole Via Francigena. It is in two volumes – the first covering the route from Canterbury and on through France and Switzerland to the Great St Bernard Pass (just slightly over half-way), and the second covering the whole of the route from the Swiss border down through Italy to Rome.

As well providing route-finding information, a description of places to visit and information on where to sleep and eat, this guide also contains suggestions for further reading in Appendix A and a list of useful addresses and websites in Appendix B. Appendices C, D and E contain, respectively, an index of sketch maps used in the guide, an index of principal place names and a summary of the route with distances.

The 1900km walk from Canterbury to Rome will take a reasonably fit person about three months, allowing for some rest days to visit places of interest along the way or simply to have a break from walking. The part of the route described in this first volume, 945km from Canterbury up to the Great St Bernard Pass at 2473m (8114ft) above sea level on the border of Switzerland and Italy,

takes six to seven weeks. As indicated above, however, the journey can be undertaken in sections, and instructions are given in the text as to how to reach (or leave) the main towns along the way. A lot of the walker's route described here is also suitable for cyclists, but they should also consult the Chinn/Gallard guide (see Appendix A).

Anyone who is thinking of walking or cycling the Via Francigena should certainly consider contacting the Confraternity of Pilgrims to Rome for advice and membership (see Appendix B for contact details).

HISTORY

People have been making pilgrimages to Rome since the fourth century when, with the Edict of Milan in AD313, the Roman Empire became Christian, unleashing a veritable flood of pilgrims anxious to visit the tombs of Saints Peter and Paul in the city. These early pilgrims were aided in their undertaking by the well-maintained infrastructure of Roman roads and the network of *mansiones* (inns for travellers) at intervals along the way, as well as by the frequent *termae* (Roman baths) to be found in many places on the route.

Gradually, however, the numbers of pilgrims swelled to such an extent that the existing accommodation no longer sufficed, and as early as the fifth century dedicated pilgrim 'hospitals' (places where hospitality was offered to travellers, both the sick and the well) began to be built. These early pilgrims had no linguistic difficulties, as they were able to convey their needs in Latin (a language later spoken only by clerics). As early as the ninth century, phrase books appeared, with the most important everyday vocabulary provided in the languages of the countries or areas the pilgrim would pass through.

However, with the Barbarian invasions of the sixth and seventh centuries, pilgrim life became much more difficult. Roads and bridges ceased to be maintained, inns and other accommodation were not kept up, and in areas no longer under Christian rule pilgrimage became increasingly dangerous, with pilgrims beset by bands of robbers, barbarian invaders and pirates during sea crossings, to say nothing of storms, wild animals, lack of food and sickness, and the pilgrim was not at all sure he would reach his destination, let alone return home in one piece.

All these trials and tribulations are well documented in writings from the sixth century onwards, and many pilgrims wrote accounts of their experiences, recounting the everyday happenings as well as the dangers of the route. One of the earliest of these was the English monk Gildas the Wise, who went to Rome in AD530. The two journeys made by Saint Wilfred, in 666 and again in 673, are also well documented, while the first 'tourist guide' to Rome, the *Salzburger Reisebuch*, was produced as early as the seventh century

Halloy (gallery), Eglise Saint-Pierre, Bar-sur-Aube (Section 4)

and listed all the places a pilgrim should be sure to visit. The *Einsiedler Manuskript* of AD750 went a step further, providing the pilgrim, in addition, with ten 'tourist walks' round the town to take in the principal sights of ancient Rome.

Sigeric and the first 'guidebook'

A detailed route description was left by the Icelandic Abbot Nikolas von Munkathverá, who travelled to Rome in 1154, via Strasbourg and Basel, to join the Via Francigena in Switzerland, but the first real 'guidebook' to the route from Canterbury – and the one which has had the greatest influence on subsequent pilgrim journeys – was made at the instigation of Sigeric, Archbishop of Canterbury, when he went to Rome in AD990.

Like all his predecessors, he went to Rome to receive his *pallium* – a white woollen stole/scarf with six black crosses on it that formed his seal of office – from the Pope. Sigeric went there with a considerable retinue, in 79 daily stages, spent 3 days in Rome, during which he dined once with the Pope and visited 23 churches, and then set off back home again. On the return journey he asked his secretary to write up a description of the route, the result of which is a list, in Latin, of these stages and where they spent the night (the manuscript is now in the British Museum).

This 'guidebook' became the basis for future journeys to Rome made by pilgrims from Britain and

places along the way, and fixed what is sometimes referred to as the 'Sigeric route', the one which has become known today as the Via Francigena. This is the route described in this book, based on the pioneering investigative work done by the AIVF (Associazione Internazionale della Via Francigena) in the mid-1990s, and includes most of the stopping places used by Sigeric – Arras, Laon, Reims, Châlons, Bar-sur-Aube, Besançon, Pontarlier, Lausanne, Martigny and so on. However, as his route used the Roman road network, most of which is now *routes nationales*, quieter, safer alternatives have been described instead. In essence, however, it is the same route as the one the late 10th-century Archbishop of Canterbury and his companions took over 1000 years ago. The numbers of his different stages (the first begins in Rome) are given in the text as you come to the place in question.

One of the first people to remedy some of the practical difficulties of this route was the Merovingian Queen Brunhilde who, towards the end of the sixth century, organized repairs to the Roman road system in her domain, from the Channel coast down to Thérouanne, Arras and beyond. Although it is now a tarred road for the most part, this route still bears the name Chaussée Brunehaut ('Brunhilde's road'), and modern pilgrims follow or shadow it for a considerable part of their journey through northern France.

Interior of church at Hospice du Grand Saint-Bernard (Section 6)

Alternative pilgrim routes

Until the beginning of the eighth century, however, the route along the Rhine was the one taken by many pilgrims journeying to Rome, but as the area was not yet under Christian rule it was extremely dangerous. The fifth-century English princess Ursula, for example, was returning home from a pilgrimage accompanied by 11 virgins (the numbers swelled to 11,000 in the legend that grew up subsequently) when she and all her retinue were murdered by the Huns as she approached Cologne. By the beginning of the eighth century, English clerics and lay pilgrims had begun to travel through the area that is now present-day France instead.

Under Charles the Great things improved dramatically, and pilgrim numbers swelled considerably, but after the end of the Carolingian period pilgrimage became dangerous again as the Saracens moved further and further west. They reached the mouth of the Tiber, threatened to destroy Rome's two most important Christian basilicas, Saint Peter's and Saint Paul-Outside-the-Walls, and invaded the whole Alpine region. Only when they were finally driven back in the 10th century did the crossing of the Alps over the Great St Bernard Pass become safe enough to use again.

While the dangers of the journey to Rome were sufficient enough to deter prospective pilgrims, the discovery, in the early ninth century, of the tomb of Saint James in north-western Spain and the establishment of the third important European pilgrimage,

17

to Santiago de Compostela, deprived Rome of its unique position of being the only city to have apostles' graves within its precincts. As the popularity of the Santiago pilgrimage rose, so the one to the tombs of Saints Peter and Paul began to decline, especially given all the practical and political difficulties of this journey.

Holy Years

However, in the year 1300 pilgrimage to Rome received an unexpected impetus when Pope Boniface VIII declared it a Jubilee (Holy) Year, during which pilgrims could receive a plenary indulgence – a complete remission of all sins, something usually obtainable only by taking part in a Crusade. There were conditions attached, and for a complete remission of all sins the pilgrim had to confess on 15 successive days in the basilicas of both Saint Peter's and Saint Paul's (unlike the ordinary citizen, who had to do so on 30 successive days).

So great was the demand for plenary indulgences that over two million pilgrims went to Rome during the Holy Year in 1300, many in large groups from Germany, France and England. The annals of the hospice at the Great St Bernard Pass for that year recorded 20,000 overnight stays, while for Rome itself the Holy Year was not only a spiritual but also a resounding business success – it was reported that pilgrim donations at the altar in Saint Peter's basilica totalled

30,000 gold florins (equivalent to £7 million today) in that year alone.

The next Holy Year was 50 years later, while in the 1400 Jubilee Year there was an outbreak of plague, and large numbers of Roman citizens and pilgrims died. However, in 1450 Pope Nicholas V took in so much gold from pilgrim donations that he was able to start rebuilding Saint Peter's and endow the Vatican Library with precious manuscripts from all over the world. After that Holy Years were declared every 25 years, and pilgrim numbers continued to rise, a pattern which continued until the Reformation, at which point pilgrimages were officially banned in all Protestant countries. Hardly any pilgrims were in evidence in Rome in 1525 and 1550, but with the Counter-Reformation numbers swelled again and Rome, with a population of 100,000 inhabitants, saw some 400,000 pilgrims arrive in 1575 and over 500,000 in 1600.

After that numbers continued to rise consistently each year until, by the end of the 19th century, the arrival of mass transportation started a change which altered the character of pilgrimage from a personal effort made under one's own steam to the phenomenon we have today, whereby large groups of people arrive quickly in Rome by bus, train or charter plane. Pilgrimages in Holy Years continued throughout the 20th century, with television and the mass media making them even better known, and in

Pilgrims on their way to Canterbury (Canterbury cathedral, west window) (Section 1)

the 2000 Jubilee Year 25 million pilgrims visited Rome by one means or another. Today's foot pilgrims have therefore swung full circle, making a conscious choice to travel under their own steam and at their own speed, on a journey in which not only the end, but also the means, are of great significance.

PILGRIMS THROUGH THE CENTURIES

Who were the pilgrims who made this often perilous journey to Rome? People from all walks of life and stratae of society, such as those depicted in the *Canterbury Tales*, more men than women (the latter were often actively discouraged from doing so on

'moral' grounds), the high-born, the low, and all those in between. Among the many prominent persons who made the journey to Rome and back (often more than once in their lifetime) were Wilfrid, Bishop of Ripon, Saint Boniface and, of course, many Archbishops of Canterbury.

But why did people go on pilgrimages? For a variety of reasons – as a profession of faith, for instance, and a quest to save their souls, as a way of acquiring merit (and thus, for example, reducing the amount of time spent in Purgatory), and as a search for healing, both mental and physical – although we know nowadays that many who felt themselves to be miraculously 'cured' were very often only in spontaneous remission due

19

to a change of diet, season, climate or place. Pilgrimages were made as a means of atonement too (certain crimes such as the murder of children or a priest could be absolved only by the Pope) or punishment. A system of fixed penalties for certain crimes or sins was in operation during the Middle Ages and a standard sentence for the murder of a bishop, for example, or one's father, the theft of church goods and arson (since almost all houses at the time were made of wood) was a pilgrimage to Rome. For others it was an opportunity to venerate the relics of saints available along way (indulgences were often available to those who visited shrines). Later there were even professional pilgrims who would (for a fee) undertake to do the pilgrimage on behalf of someone else who could afford the money but not the time to do it him or herself.

There were some, too, who were just glad of the opportunity to escape their surroundings – from a sense of adventure, or perhaps to shirk family responsibilities. And there were others with very definite ulterior motives – thieves, vagabonds, heretics, army deserters and *coquillards* (pseudo-pilgrims, so named because they would wear the *coquille* or scallop shell to disguise their intentions along the pilgrim road to Santiago) – all of whom were out to exploit the true pilgrim, to rob, steal, and take advantage of the alms and accommodation available along the way. Those with the means to do so went on horseback,

and some wealthy people made the pilgrimage along with a considerable retinue (Kaiser Friedrich II, for example, is reported to have made the journey in the 13th century accompanied not only by a multitude of servants but 25 camels, five leopards and an elephant!). The majority of pilgrims went on foot, however, and even among the rich there were some who preferred to walk, rather than ride, because of the greater merit they would attain.

Preparing for pilgrimage

Pilgrims were not at all sure that they would reach their destination, let alone return home in one piece, so

Signpost with pilgrim logo, near Saint-Maurice (Section 6)

before setting out (those with honourable motives, at least) they took leave of their family and employer, made their will, gave a generous donation to the poor, and generally put their affairs in order. They obtained their credential (pilgrim passport) from their bishop or church, which could then be presented in order to obtain food and lodging in the many pilgrim hospitals and other establishments along the way and be stamped there as they went along. This was both a precaution against the growing number of coquillards and a means of furnishing evidence, if needed, that they had made the pilgrimage successfully.

Pilgrims had their staff (normally some 2m long and fitted with an iron spike at the end, useful not only to walk with but as a defence against dogs and wild animals) and scrip (small knapsack) blessed in church before setting out. (This ceremony is thought to have originated in the blessing of knights before they left for the First Crusade).

They travelled light, carrying little else but a gourd for water. Both male and female pilgrims were easily recognizable by the heavy cloak they wore, made of untreated wool and reasonably waterproof, which also served as a blanket at night. Male pilgrims wore wide-brimmed hats, women a shawl or scarf, and both normally walked in sturdy lace-up boots or stout sandals. (Contrary to popular belief, barefoot pilgrims were the exception.)

And to distinguish themselves from pilgrims to other destinations, those making their way to Rome had,

Abbaye de Saint-Maurice (Section 6)

Canterbury cathedral (Section 1)

on the metal badge they wore stitched to their hat or cloak, either the crossed keys of Saint Peter or the 'Veronica' (the representation of Christ's face on the cloth with which Saint Veronica wiped his face on the way to his death on the cross).

Accommodation

Pilgrims with funds could stay in inns and other publicly available lodgings, but the vast majority probably stayed in the different hospices (lodgings for travellers, usually run by religious orders) and other facilities provided especially for them. Some of these were in towns (either in the centre, or outside the walls to cater both for latecomers and possibly contagious pilgrims), while others were in the countryside, often by bridges or at the

crossing of important pilgrim feeder roads – at Canterbury, for example, Laon, Rosnay l'Hôpital, Villeneuve, Saint-Maurice and the Hospice at the Great St Bernard Pass.

Much of this pilgrim accommodation was provided by religious orders (who also tended those who were sick and looked after them until they were well enough to set out on their journey again), as well as by churches, civic authorities and benevolent individuals. The facilities offered varied considerably from one establishment to another, but surviving records from many of them indicate exactly what was provided for the pilgrim.

Routes to Rome

The Via Francigena as described here is not (and never was) the one and only 'real' pilgrim road to Rome, but simply one of many taken by those who came from Britain or places along the way. Pilgrims from the Iberian Peninsula, for example, would have followed the coast through southern France, while those from other parts of France would have crossed the Alps not by the Great St Bernard but by the Montcenis or Montgenèvre passes. Germans and those from further afield may well have taken the Brenner or St Gothard passes into Italy, while others made their way overland to Venice and from there to Rome. And there were other routes, too, taken by pilgrims approaching the Eternal City from the south, some of which are being cleared and investigated today.

A whole network of routes converged on Rome and the journey began, at least until the 20th century, from each and every pilgrim's own front door. As the well-known saying goes, 'all roads lead to Rome'.

PILGRIM SAINTS

Saint Francis of Assisi is known to have made the pilgrimage to Rome many times, as well as to Santiago de Compostela and Jerusalem, and Saint Christopher (frequently represented carrying a child on his shoulder) is well known as the patron saint of travellers in general. However, the real patron saint of pilgrims is Saint Roch (in French and English, San Rocco in Italian) and is the one most in evidence on the Via Francigena in Italy.

Born in Montpellier in the south of France he made a pilgrimage to Rome, after which he stayed in Italy and devoted his life to caring for plague victims in Acquapendente. However, when he contracted a disease himself, which left him with an unsightly sore on his left thigh, he withdrew to live in isolation in a forest.

For this reason Saint Roch is depicted in art with the front flap of his coat turned back, to warn people to keep away from him, and is accompanied sometimes by a small child or an angel, but always by the faithful dog, often with a loaf of bread in his mouth, who is said to have brought the saint his daily rations stolen from his master's table in a large house nearby. Legend has confused Saint Roch with Santiago Peregrino (Saint James the pilgrim) at times, and he not infrequently appears in a 'pilgrim version' as well, with added hat, staff and scallop shells on his clothing. In Italy, in particular, you will see many representations of him in churches and chapels along the way and on frescoes on their exteriors.

Saint Peter

Those who have made the journey to Santiago de Compostela, particularly along the Camino Francés, will have been struck by the number of churches and chapels dedicated to Saint James along the way in Spain and by the numerous statues, stained-glass windows, paintings and other representations of the saint in his different guises. By contrast, pilgrims

23

Below *Stained-glass window with Saint Peter, Eglise Saint-Pierre, Bar-sur-Aube (Section 4)*

Above *Stained-glass window of Saint Peter, Bourg Saint-Pierre church (Section 6)*

Above *Statue of Saint Peter, Eglise Saint-Pierre, Bar-sur-Aube (Section 4)*

who make the journey to Rome will not find the same number of references to Saint Peter along the Via Francigena, even though the object of many pilgrimages was to visit his tomb in the Basilica in Rome. There are a number of churches and chapels dedicated to Saint Peter (Saint-Pierre) on the Via Francigena in Britain, France and Switzerland, but these are so named because this has always been a popular church dedication, in many countries, and not because they were on an important Christian pilgrimage route. Where known the presence of these is indicated in the text, as are representations of Saint Peter in sculpture, stained glass and so on. There are also one or two

churches along the way dedicated to Saint-Pierre-aux-Liens (Saint Peter in Chains), referring to the chains that bound him while he was imprisoned in Jerusalem and which were preserved aftwards as relics.

Pilgrims with a particular interest in iconography will find him represented chiefly as an older person, frequently, although not always, seated, and recognisable by his keys (to the Kingdom of Heaven). He is also often portrayed accompanied by the model of a boat (recalling the fact that he was a fisherman before he became an apostle) or by a cockerel, reminding the viewer of Peter's threefold denial of Christ after the crucifixion. More is known about the life of Saint Peter than of any of the other apostles; it is recorded (in the Apocryphal New Testament), for example, that his martyrdom took place by crucifixion – but upside down, so as not to be equated with his master

This has been a very brief introduction to a vast subject, just enough to put modern pilgrims 'in the picture' and provide some background to their undertaking (for more information see Appendix A). For a general introduction to pilgrimage the Sumption book is highly recommended, and for the Via Francigena in particular the book by Zweidler is excellent, but only available in German. An equally excellent (shorter) introduction to the history and places along this route by Jean-Yves Grégoire was published in early 2010, in French. There is unfortunately, at present, at least, nothing even remotely equivalent available in English.

GEOGRAPHY

From **Canterbury** to Dover the Via Francigena follows the North Downs Way (coinciding in part with both the Elham Valley Way and Cycle Track 16), with its rolling landscapes, small picturesque villages set in farmland, with red brick cottages, the occasional oast house and several Norman churches. Until you reach Dover there is only one place en route (Shepherdswell, also known as Sibertswold) where you can get anything to eat or drink and the majority of the walking in this section is on footpaths.

From **Dover**, now somewhat run-down and a shadow of its former self, the modern pilgrim takes the ferry across the Channel to **Calais**, although in centuries gone by Wissant, 20km further west, was the shortest crossing point. This was the harbour used until, following severe storms in the 18th century, the town was submerged under sand on two occasions. After that Calais became the principal port of entry into northern France.

Once on the other side, the modern pilgrim can chose between 'turning right' along the coast to **Wissant** and then 'hard left' to reach **Guînes** (where Henry VIII met the French king François I on the Field of the Cloth of Gold), which is 36km along two sides of an isosceles triangle, or going straight to Guînes along the canal (only 12km). In either case much of the route in this part of France is fairly flat and a lot of the walking on (very quiet) minor roads, the largely arable landscape punctuated with small villages whose church towers can be seen in the distance.

Once again there are hardly any facilities such as shops and cafés and there are also very few places to sit down and eat, rest or take cover from the rain, as the churches do not have porches accessible from the outside and there are few seats or benches in public places. For this reason readers will find references in the guide (which may initially surprise them) indicating where bus shelters are located.

Northern and north-eastern France were formerly a prosperous **coal-mining area** (readers of Zola's *Germinal* will find this familiar), with *terrils* (pointed slag heaps) and *corons* (miners' cottages, usually in terraces) built by the mining companies for their employees and characteristic of the area around Divion. Today, however, nearly all the mines are closed and the whole area is very depressed, with high levels of unemployment.

After that, still shadowing the Chaussée Brunehaut, the Via Francigena makes its way to **Arras**, a town noted for its wall tapestries in medieval times (hence the expression 'behind the arras'). It was completely flattened by German bombing in the two world wars, but rebuilt, with the help of archival photographs, as a replica of the original. This area is characterised by its *beffrois* (tall, *campanile*-style bell-towers on public buildings), Flemish-style houses and, everywhere from here onwards and throughout the whole of the *départment* of the Somme and beyond, military cemeteries attesting to the phenomenal carnage of both the First and Second World Wars.

The modern pilgrim cannot fail to notice the **cemeteries**. Those in which the Commonwealth and Allied soldiers were buried have row upon row of identical gravestones, frequently planted with flowers, in contrast to the stark rows of black iron crosses in the German cemeteries, covered over with grass and with very few trees around. Some of these *nécropoles* (literally 'cities of the dead') are enormous and stretch for several square miles; others are very small, with only a couple of dozen graves, like the 'Sunken Road' and 'Manchester' cemeteries on the roadside south of Bapaume. These were often located on the site of field hospitals – the dead buried, almost literally, where they had fallen. These are all extremely well looked after both by the War

British cemetery, Rancourt (Section 3)

Mairie at Bar-sur-Aube (Section 4)

Graves Commission and the Société des Anciens Combattants, and all have a register available to help visitors identify individual graves.

Péronne is another town whose centre has been completely rebuilt, after which the route continues through the arable land of the Vermandois to **Tergnier** (a big railway junction), where the landscape becomes hillier and more wooded, and leads the pilgrim to the hilltop cathedral town of **Laon**. From there the pilgrim walks on to **Reims**, with its famous cathedral, and the start of the Champagne region, with vineyards to either side of the route, stretching to infinity. From there it continues along the Canal Latéral à la Marne, for the most part, to **Châlons-en-Champagne**. After that the Via

Francigena goes along the straight-as-a-die Chaussée Brunehaut to **Brienne-le-Château**, with its Ecole Militaire where Napoléon did his training. Up to this point you may have met other pilgrims – but probably bound for Santiago, not Rome. German, Belgian, Dutch and other pilgrims heading for Santiago, who start from their respective countries, join your route north of Arras and keep company with you until shortly after Brienne-la-Vielle, after which they 'peel off' to the right to join the Vézelay route a day or two later and part company with you.

From Brienne-le-Château the route continues to **Bar-sur-Aube**, past the former Abbaye de Clairvaux, set in the woods, now one of France's biggest top-security prisons, to the old fortified town of **Châteauvillain** with its celebrated deer park, the Parc aux Daims. After that it passes through undulating wooded landscapes to the hilltop cathedral town of **Langres**, birthplace of Diderot and known for its cutlery and wickerwork manufacture. The route then leaves the département of the Haute-Marne to enter the Haute-Saône and, with it, the old province of the Franche-Comté, with its numerous *lavoirs*, communal outdoor laundry facilities.

The **lavoirs** typically consist of two large interconnected purpose-built pools, one higher than the other, and with water running continuously through the upper one (used for rinsing) to the lower (for washing). In this part of France they were normally under a roof, with seating down at least one side, and in the past served as a focal point of village life and gossip. Today many are still working, although little used, while others, dried up, provide useful cover from sun or rain for the pilgrim seeking a quiet rest. There are variations on this theme in the form of *lavoirs-flottants* (with a moveable floor – there is one in Châteauvillain, for example) and the *mairie-lavoir*, like the one in Dampierre-sur-Salon. The latter type of building was constructed over a small river, with the *mairie* (town hall) and all its administrative offices upstairs on the first floor, and the washing facilities, open to the public at all times, underneath at ground level.

The other noticeable feature of the Franche-Comté region is its churches with **decorative roofs** known as *clochers comtois* (or *clochers à l'impériale*). The domed roofs of their bell-towers

Washing facility part of mairie-lavoir, Dampierre-sur-Salon (Section 4)

are covered in brightly coloured ceramic tiles in various criss-cross patterns. Each one is slightly different in both colour and design, and of the more than 700 examples in the region you will see many in towns and villages along the course of the Via Francigena in this part of France.

The Via Francigena goes on again, into the départment of the Doubs and to **Besançon**, set in a tongue of land surrounded by the river and with its characteristic yellow-and-blue stone buildings. After that the route becomes increasingly hilly as it approaches **Pontarlier**, after which it climbs up to **Les Fourgs** and crosses the border into Switzerland at **La Grande Borne** (1108m). The route heads down to **Sainte-Croix**, across flat wooded countryside, to the spa town of **Yverdon-les-Bains** on the southern shore of Lake Neuchâtel and from there, through more woods and agricultural land, goes down, down and down to **Lausanne** on the shores of Lac Leman (Lake Geneva). Here the Via Francigena crosses the Camino de Santiago coming from Einsiedeln and places further east, and here again you may encounter pilgrims from Germany, Austria and other parts of Switzerland bound for Santiago de Compostela rather than Rome.

At Lausanne, the route continues alongside the lake, close to the water's edge in the main, and with Switzerland's biggest vineyard area – the Côtes de Lavaux – on the slopes above to your left. It goes through

Vevey, a tourist town since the 18th century and home for many years to many famous artists, musicians, painters and so on, including Charlie Chaplin, Oskar Kokoschka, Fyodor Dostoevsky, Victor Hugo, Vladimir Nabokov, Noel Coward and AJ Cronin. This area, known as the Swiss Riviera, continues past **Montreux**, with its casino and sumptuous residences of the well-to-do reaching down to the water's edge. The town developed only in the 19th century when the British, in particular, were looking for places to stay when on holiday.

The walking here is all on tarmac, but there is a lot of shade, as well as trees and flower beds everywhere – and plenty of seats! Before you get to the end of the lake the route passes the Château de Chillon, Switzerland's most visited tourist attraction, built on a sort of semi-island – its fortress side faces the shore, and its princely-residence aspect looks out over the lake. After **Villeneuve** the route turns inland, up the Rhône valley to **Aigle**, with its belt of arable land and industrial estates wedged in between the mountains to either side. It heads gradually uphill all the time until it reaches Saint-Maurice d'Aguane with its nearly 1500-year-old abbey that has never closed since it opened in AD515, overshadowed by the mountains of the Dents du Midi.

Martigny is next (471m), with the valley getting narrower and narrower and the mountains closing in to either side as the route climbs steadily

Looking up the valley, near Orsières (Section 6)

up to **Sembrancher** (717m), with its old streets lined with *raccards*, old wooden barn-like houses used for storing grain. From there it takes the Chemin Napoléon along the side of the valley up to **Orsières** (901m), from where it continues up through the woods to Liddes (1346m), after which the trees begin to thin out. The route continues on again past the Barrage de Toules (a big dam) with Alpine meadows, a paradise of wild flowers in the springtime, and the high summer pasture lands. It goes up and up again to **Bourg Saint-Pierre** (1632m), the last populated place before the St Bernard Pass, with several interesting vernacular buildings.

After this the route follows the increasingly steep climb up to **L'Hospitalet** (2120m) and then the final stretch up the rocky Combe des

Morts (Valley of the Dead) to the **Col du Grand Saint-Bernard**, the Great St Bernard Pass, at 2473m (8114ft) above sea level. Its hospice has been in existence for nearly 1000 years, putting up pilgrims and other travellers, and has never closed its doors in all that time.

You will see snow on the peaks all year round, but even as late as July you may find a lot on the paths and tracks after L'Hospitalet and, not being able to judge its depth, need to have recourse to the road in unsuitable weather. On a brilliant sunny day, however, regardless of the temperature, the views are fantastic, mountains all round you with their rocky slopes and only the lake, often iced over, even in summer, separating you from the next stage of your experience – Italy.

PREPARING FOR YOUR JOURNEY

Read up as much as you can about the route – its history, art, architecture and geography – as well as other people's accounts of their journeys. Suggestions for further reading are given in Appendix A, but there is not a great deal of information about the route (as opposed to the individual places) in English at present. However, the Confraternity of Pilgrims to Rome's *Newsletter* has some interesting articles on various aspects of the pilgrimage, as does also the twice-yearly (bilingual – Italian and English) *Via Francigena* magazine.

If you are not used to walking or carrying a rucksack day in, day out, or have not already walked (without back-up transport) other long-distance routes, then make sure you get in plenty of practice before you go. Consider joining your local rambling club at least six months in advance and go out with them as often as you can. Most clubs have walks of different lengths and speeds so you can start with shorter, slower ones if you need to, and gradually build up your speed and stamina. In this way you can benefit from walking with other people and having someone to lead who knows the way and suitable places to go, and you can also practise walking in hilly places (which you will need).

Then start increasing the amount you take out with you until you can carry what you need. After that go out walking on at least two consecutive days on several occasions, in hilly places, carrying all your proposed gear with you – walking 30km on a 'one-off' basis is a very different matter from getting up again the following morning, probably stiff and possibly footsore, and starting out all over again. With this kind of preparation, you should have an enjoyable journey, with trouble-free feet and back. Remember too, however, that a lot of the route through France and Switzerland is on tarmac (which will be hot in summer), so get in plenty of practice on this type of surface too, as well as on stony tracks and loose gravel.

Once you have crossed the Channel and arrived in Calais don't expect anybody – anybody at all – to speak English! Assume you will have to speak French all the time (or Italian, if you continue beyond Switzerland, although the Valle d'Aosta is bilingual) for everything you need, however

Explanatory notice in Bourg Saint-Pierre – in French, naturally! (Section 6)

complicated. So if you are not already fairly fluent, consider a year's evening classes or home study with tapes in your preparations – you will find yourself extremely isolated if you are unable to carry out practical transactions and converse with the many local people you will meet along the way. And make sure that, even if you don't achieve much else, you have mastered the numbers and can recognize them at speed in prices, distances, telephone numbers, and so on.

Note Although you may have learned that the number 70 is 'soixante-dix' in French, 80 is 'quatre-vingts', 90 is 'quatre-vingt-dix', 91 'quatre-vingt-onze' and so on, in Switzerland the terms 'septante', 'huitante' and 'nonante' are used, respectively, for 70, 80 and 90. Therefore 72 will be 'septante-deux', 89 'huitante-neuf' and so on – something you will need to get used to in shops, for example.

Decide what type of footwear you will be taking – walking shoes, lightweight boots, heavy (thick-soled) trainers, and so on – and break them in well before you go.

Pack your rucksack well ahead of your departure, leave out anything which 'might come in useful' and which you would only be using occasionally, and remember that you will have to allow space for food and water, especially in the section through France.

CHOOSING YOUR COMPANIONS

Two-legged

Unlike the busy Camino de Santiago the Via Francigena at present, and especially in the section through France, is definitely not a route for people who cannot cope with extended periods of their own

Path near Martigny (Section 6)

company. So, unless you plan to go with someone you already know well and have walked with before, think very carefully about any companion you might consider going with, especially if you feel that you would rather go with anyone else rather than be alone. (In Italian there is an expression which reminds you to be alert to the possible dangers – 'Meglio soli che male accompagnati' – better alone than in unsuitable company.)

Some issues are obvious. Does the other person walk at the same speed as you, for example, or manage the same daily distances? Others, however, are less so. Consider, for example:

- do you prefer to walk nonstop until you reach your daily destination, or take rests and sit down to admire the view?
- do you get up at the crack of dawn and start immediately or find it difficult to get going in the morning?
- do you want to stay in hotels or in pilgrim refuges, parish accommodation, youth hostels or other economical accommodation?
- do you enjoy eating out in restaurants or doing your own cooking where possible?
- do you/your companion speak fluent French while the other one is monolingual English?
- does one of you chatter nonstop all day long while the other prefers to walk mainly in silence?

- do you – something that is often overlooked until it is too late – have the same level of funds available as the other person?

Some of these issues can make or mar a pilgrim journey in the constant company of another person. It will help, though, if you discuss these issues in advance.

Four-legged

Do not be tempted to take your dog with you.

- You will meet local dogs along the way who are on their own territory and do not take kindly to strange ones.
- Hardly any accommodation of any type, except campsites, accepts them.
- You may have transport problems returning home.
- Most dogs, although used to going out all day long, are not accustomed to continuous long-distance walking and may experience problems with their feet.

Saint Bernard puppy – a dog that does belong on the trail!

TACKLING THE VIA IN ONE TRIP

If you can, do consider making the whole journey in one go – an experience you are unlikely to repeat that takes, on average, three months. There's no need to make your will, as did pilgrims of old, but certain practical matters will need attention before departure to ensure you can 'switch off' while you're away. (Make sure you've paid any important monthly bills up front or put enough money in an account to do so automatically while you're away.) Choose your companions carefully and remember, while packing, that you will be walking in two different seasons. (You will need to set off some time between Easter and early August.) Finally, make sure you give yourself enough 'debriefing space' on return before returning to your normal routine.

PLANNING YOUR PILGRIMAGE

The route through Britain, France and Switzerland is practicable for much of the year, although not necessarily recommended, but under no circumstances should you consider crossing the Great St Bernard Pass in winter. It is usually free from snow from late May to late September, although snowfalls can occur at night even during July and August (and snow remain during the day), so if you are intending to make the pilgrimage from Canterbury to Rome in a single journey you will have to take this into

An attractive sundial in Lausanne, a good place for a rest day (Section 5)

account in your planning. As a result, however, of aiming for the warmer months, the weather will be very hot when you get to Italy.

Canterbury to the Great St Bernard Pass can be walked comfortably in six to seven weeks by anyone who is fairly fit, and this includes plenty of time to visit places of interest along the way. Be generous with your timings when planning your itinerary, especially if you are not an experienced walker. Start with fairly short stages, if accommodation allows, and always stop before you are tired. You can increase the distances as you get fitter and into the swing of things. In addition, allow plenty of time and flexibility for unforeseen circumstances (pleasant or otherwise).

It is advisable to include short days and rest days in your schedule – where and how many is up to you. On a short walking day you can arrive at your destination during the late morning, ideally, and have the remainder of the day completely free. However, because of the lack of accommodation in France, it is difficult to include such short days in your programme, so you will probably need to take a whole day off if you want to have a rest. If you are extremely tired, or having trouble with your feet, a complete day off works wonders (particularly in a small place with no sights to be visited), and is well worth the disruption to your schedule that it might initially seem to entail. If you enjoy sight-seeing, on the other hand, consider taking days off in Arras, Reims, Besançon and Lausanne, as well as at the Great St Bernard Pass.

A CHALLENGING PILGRIM ROUTE

Many of those, although by no means all, who decide to walk the Via Francigena today have already made the pilgrimage to Santiago de Compostela, usually along the route from the Pyrenees known as the Camino Francés. This section is intended to alert such pilgrims to the contrasting natures of the two routes.

On the Via Francigena, in France, until you get down towards Besançon and the Swiss border, there aren't many 'ups and downs' on the route, but distances between accommodation, especially of the economical kind, are often extremely long (for walkers). There are hardly any useful facilities along the way in this part of France either. While there are plenty of villages, very few of them have a shop, a bar, a restaurant or a water fountain, and you may well go for two days at a time (before Arras, for example, and after Châlons-en-Champagne) without seeing any of these, so careful organization is required to ensure that you have something to eat (as well as drink) when you need it.

On the Camino Francés, if you have the time or are unfit, you need walk only 10km (or even less) each day to find accommodation (often inexpensive) and services and facilities at frequent intervals along the way. On the Via Francigena, on the other hand, you will need to be fit before you start, especially in northern France. Unless you take a tent (campsites are plentiful) or have a back-up vehicle you need to be able to walk long distances with a heavy rucksack, especially if you are doing the journey on a tight budget.

On the Camino Francés you can turn up at a refuge (usually open and waiting for you) and frequently find another English-speaking pilgrim to 'show you the ropes', even if the person in charge of the establishment speaks only Spanish. You will also frequently find plenty of other pilgrims to talk to. On the Via Francigena, on the other hand, you need a reasonable level of French to cope with the mechanics of finding accommodation, especially if this involves phoning ahead. However, in contrast to the Camino Francés, where pilgrims are now so commonplace as to no longer attract the attention of local people, on the Via Francigena you do meet people who are curious to know where you are going, what you are doing (and often why), and who like to chat to you. If your linguistic skills are up to it, this can be a very enjoyable and enriching part of your experience. So unless you stay exclusively in the kind of up-market establishments where you can book everything up in advance on the internet you will need enough French to do more than 'get by' ordering food and drink. The parish accommodation in France and Switzerland, for example, needs prior (and tactful) telephone contact.

You are very unlikely to meet any other pilgrims going to Rome on the Via Francigena at present so there is hardly ever the 'fraternity of the road' that exists along the Camino Francés, where you get to know people as you go along, so you need to be very self-reliant if you decide to walk to Rome. The hardest part of the whole enterprise is not, however, the actual walking, but the mental effort needed to find somewhere to sleep, night after night after night, especially if you are doing the journey on a tight budget. It can often be difficult to remember that you are a pilgrim, too, on the Via Francigena at present, and not just a walker, as not only are you on your own much or all of the way. Even if you go to church or stay in religious houses from time to time there are no dedicated pilgrim masses, other services or pilgrim discussion groups as there are, increasingly, on the Camino Francés.

Hotel/pension-type accommodation in France and Switzerland is more expensive than in Spain, and there is a near absence of dedicated pilgrim accommodation on the Via Francigena. In addition, you rarely find the bar-restaurants with rooms that you often encounter along the route in Spain. There is no equivalent of the very good-value all-inclusive Spanish *menú del día* in either France or Switzerland and very few places at present where you can do your own cooking.

There is a very great deal more road walking on the Via Francigena than there is on the Camino Francés where, for the benefit of both pilgrims and other road-users, much of the Camino has been re-routed onto newly cleared old tracks and paths. It is therefore, at present, at least, more difficult to 'switch off' as you walk along the Via Francigena, even in Switzerland where, for the most part, the route is well waymarked. In France, where it is unwaymarked, you need your map in your hand all the time.

One other way in which the two pilgrimage routes differ, and already mentioned above, is the paucity, on the road to Rome, and through France and Switzerland in particular, of anything comparable to the very extensive Jacobean iconography to be found on

Road between Vuillecins and Pontarlier (Section 5) – there is a great deal more road walking on the Via Francigena than on the Camino Francés

the Camino Francés. In Italy you will find numerous depictions of the patron saint of pilgrims, San Rocco – statues, friezes, paintings and so on – but almost no examples before then.

So why, the reader might well be wondering, given all these difficulties, would anyone actually want to walk to Rome? There are naturally all sorts of reasons, ranging from the sheer physical challenge of such a lengthy undertaking, through cultural and historic considerations to spiritual aspects in the widest sense. There is also the build-up of inner strength that takes place as one day unfolds before the next – seeing new places, meeting new people, the simplicity of life on a *camino* pared down to its bare essentials, solitude. Each or a combination of them will be personal to each pilgrim.

EQUIPMENT

What to take

- **Passport**
- **EHIC** (European Health Insurance Card)
- **Rucksack** At least 50 litres capacity if carrying a sleeping bag
- **Footwear** Both to walk in and a spare pair of lightweight trainers/sandals. (*Tip for cold weather* – wear sock-liners or trainer socks inside your main pair of socks to keep your feet warm, but without the added bulk of two sets of cuffs round your ankles.)
- **Waterproofs** Even in summer it may rain, but a poncho (a cape with a hood and space inside for a rucksack) is far more useful

(and far less hot) than a cagoule or anorak

- **Pullover or fleece jacket** Parts of the route are high up and it can get cold at night, even in summer
- **Scarf and gloves** according to season
- **Sun hat** Preferably with wide brim
- **Sun glasses**
- **Sleeping bag** Essential if you are camping or staying in *gîtes d'étape* or parish-type accommodation
- **Thin pillowcase** Useful in parish-type accommodation (or tent) to hold clothes when pillows are not provided
- **Sleeping mat** Essential if camping and a good precaution if sleeping in parish-type accommodation, where mattresses are not always provided
- **Towel** Essential if you are camping or staying in gîtes d'étape, youth hostels or parish-type accommodation
- **Ear plugs** Essential if sleeping in dormitory/communal accommodation
- **First aid kit** (including a needle for draining blisters). The type of elastoplast sold by the metre is more useful than individual dressings. Scissors. High-factor sunscreen if you burn easily. Crêpe bandage.
- **Torch**

- **Large water bottle** At least 2 litres capacity if walking in July and August
- **Stick** Useful for fending off/ frightening dogs and testing boggy terrain
- **Guidebook**
- **Maps**
- **Compass**
- **Small dictionary/phrase book** Unless your French is good
- **Mug, spoon, plate and knife**

If you have to have a hot drink in the morning a **Camping Gaz-type stove** is a great advantage, even though it will add extra weight to your luggage. Alternatively, if you just want to heat water for a drink, an electric plunger/ mini-boiler type of heater (with continental adapter) is useful.

A **tent** is worth taking if you intend to camp regularly (useful in France in particular), but not if you will use it only occasionally. However, you can walk the entire route from Canterbury to Rome without one, provided that you can walk long distances (up to 40km a day, although this will not happen all that often). If you do take a tent you will also need a Camping Gaz-type stove, or similar, and a good sleeping bag and mat.

In general, travel as light as you can, not just for the weight but because of the hills and, according to the season, the heat.

What not to take

- Anything 'that might just come in useful'
- Too many spare changes of clothing
- Reading matter unassociated with the pilgrimage
- Shampoo/toiletries in large or glass bottles

GETTING THERE

To destinations in the UK from London

Canterbury By bus (National Express) from London (Victoria Coach Station, frequent service); by train (frequent service) from London Victoria to Canterbury East

Dover By bus (National Express) from London (Victoria Coach Station, frequent service); by train from London Charing Cross or London Bridge (frequent service), or from London St Pancras (expensive)

To destinations in France and Switzerland

Calais The only ferry company offering a foot-passenger service is P&O Ferries (www.poferries.com), crossing time approximately 90mins

Arras By train from Paris and Lille

Reims By train from Amiens and Paris

Chalôns-en-Champagne By train from Paris

Langres By train (from Paris via Dijon)

Besançon By train from Paris

Pontarlier By bus from Besançon and train from Paris

Lausanne By train from Geneva (direct flights – there from several UK airports); TGV from Paris

Martigny By train from Geneva and Lausanne; by bus (June–Sept only) from the Great St Bernard Pass

Great St Bernard Pass Buses from both Martigny and Aosta (June–Sept only)

Aosta By train to Turin and then to Milan, Rome, etc. By 'pullman' (long-distance coach service) to Milan.

ACCOMMODATION

There are different types of accommodation available along the route – campsites, *gîtes d'étape*, youth hostels/Foyers des Jeunes Travailleurs (FJT), *chambres d'hôte* (the French equivalent of bed and breakfast in mainly country areas, often marked 'BnB' in brochures in Switzerland) and hotels. There is hardly any dedicated pilgrim accommodation as yet on the section from Canterbury to the Great St Bernard Pass.

Most towns, even small, and especially those on a river, have a **campsite**. These vary in price according to the facilities they offer, but as more and more sites are being upgraded it may not be much cheaper to camp than to stay in a gîte d'étape or youth hostel, when and where they are available. The only real advantage in carrying a tent is the freedom to stop when you want, as campsites are so numerous. Most are closed in winter (late Oct to Easter), but opening times, where

Trefcon gîte (Section 3)

known, are indicated in the text. Some campsites in France have caravans or mobile homes that they rent out per person per night, normally with cooking facilities, and in Switzerland it is worth enquiring whether they have a dormitory as well.

There are very few **gîtes d'étape** along the route in France, as most of it passes through areas that are not typical walking country, and you'll certainly not see many until you approach Besançon. These offer simple, dormitory-type accommodation, at least one hot shower and often (but not always) cooking facilities (these are indicated with a 'K' in the text where known). Blankets are usually provided, so you should only need a sheet sleeping bag. **Youth hostels**, on the other hand, are slightly more numerous, usually in big towns,

and some of those in France double up as Foyers des Jeunes Travailleurs (hostels for young workers) or are classified as Centres Internationaux de Séjour (CIS, up-market hostels), but not many offer self-catering facilities. France has two youth hostel organizations, the LFAJ and the FUAJ (with more numerous hostels) – see Appendix B for details. There are also youth hostels (which include a copious breakfast) in Lausanne and Montreux/Territet on the Swiss section of the route, plus backpackers hostels (with cooking facilities) in Yverdon-les-Bains, Lausanne and Vevey.

There are a number of **chambres d'hôte** along the way (abbreviated as 'CH' in the text), but they rarely offer an evening meal as the majority of their customers are not walkers but people who arrive in cars and so can drive to the nearest town to eat. Many have only one or two rooms, so advance booking is essential. You will also see, in country areas in Switzerland, private houses offering rooms with a 'Chambres/Zimmer' sign outside.

Hotels in France have been reclassified fairly recently ('NN' after their name/rating = *nouvelles normes*) and now have no star ratings higher than three, although '5-star'-type accommodation is available. Hotels in Switzerland are classified with star ratings of 1–5 (the same applies to B&Bs) plus an extra category at the top-end – 'unique'. Some hotels in mountain areas in Switzerland also have dormitories for walkers, and these are indicated in the text where known. In general the hotels indicated in this guide are of the more economical kind and star ratings are shown with asterisks (*).

There are, in addition, some **religious houses** in both France and Switzerland willing to accommodate pilgrims and provide meals if required. Some have a fixed charge while others operate on a donation basis, and although you will not be required to attend services you may feel it is courteous to do so.

At the bottom end of the scale there is also the possibility, in some places in France in particular, if you have a valid credential (pilgrim passport) and enough French to negotiate tactfully, to avail yourself of spartan **accommodation offered by certain parishes**. A few have a rota of people willing to put up pilgrims in their houses, but in the main you will be sleeping in a church hall, on the floor either with or without a mattress, with access to a toilet and wash basin but not necessarily a shower. You will need to telephone the parish office two or three days ahead as these only operate limited opening hours (just two mornings a week, for example), and as most priests nowadays have a large number of parishes you will rarely find that the office is in the place you want to sleep. Most do not charge, but you should always offer to leave a donation (or put something in the box if they refuse), and remember that other pilgrims will be coming after you – the way you behave will influence the reception subsequent pilgrims receive.

In almost every case, apart from campsites, you will need to phone ahead for accommodation (see 'Telephones' below) so that, apart from the stretch from Canterbury to Dover, a reasonable level of spoken French will be necessary. It is usually enough to do so one or two days ahead, and in this way you are not tied down to too rigid a timetable, leaving no flexibility for unforeseen circumstances. It is possible, of course, and some people do this, to book up every single night's accommodation in advance all the way from Canterbury to Rome as most hotels, chambres d'hôte and youth hostels now have internet facilities, but this tends to both limit you to the more expensive kind of accommodation and tie you down to an inflexible schedule.

Prices have not been indicated for each individual entry in the guide, but in general, in 2010, hotels in France cost between 50€ and 70€ for a double room (without breakfast), and in Switzerland 80–100CHF (frequently including breakfast). Chambres d'hôte are slightly less expensive, while prices in youth hotels vary according to whether you are in a dormitory or double room.

PLANNING THE DAY

In France and Switzerland there are many places worth visiting along the route of artistic, architectural, cultural or religious interest, and they are open at convenient times for the walker – usually 10am–12pm and 4pm or 5pm–7pm.

In July and August in particular it can be extremely hot during the day, in both France and Switzerland, with temperatures well up into the 90s (F) or high 30s (C). When walking in hot weather it is important to avoid becoming dehydrated by drinking plenty of water before you feel thirsty, as once you realise you haven't had enough to drink it is too late to do anything about it, even if you have supplies with you. (Top up your water bottle whenever you can.)

If you can drink at least half a litre of water as soon as you get up in the morning (as well as any tea or coffee available) you will find the hot weather affects you much less. The best way to avoid walking in the heat

is to get up before it is light and set out, if you can, at daybreak.

It is also a good idea, in large towns and other places of any size, to go for a walk in the evening and check how you will leave, so as not to waste time or get lost the following morning. And it is always useful to read through the following day's walk the night before!

OTHER PRACTICAL INFORMATION

Road numbering In France motorways are indicated with an 'A' for 'autoroute'; *routes nationales* are large main roads organised on a national scale and numbered with an 'N' (for example, N57); and less major roads organised on a regional basis (the *routes départmentales* (eg D288). These are often very busy and are the equivalent of the more important B roads in Britain.

More minor roads in France (marked with a 'C') are organised on a local basis, as are the *chemins vicinaux* (CV), the smallest minor roads. In Switzerland, on the other hand, apart from on motorways, you will not see road numbers on signposts – just the names of the places the roads serve.

Road walking Walk on the left-hand side of the road, facing any oncoming traffic, except where a sharp bend prevents you from being seen.

Railways The national railway network is known in France as SNCF and in the French-speaking part of Switzerland as CFF. In France a high-speed train is referred to as a TGV.

Accueil You will see signs for this in churches and other buildings. It means – welcome, reception desk, staff on duty or similar.

Public holidays In France (*jours fériés*): 1 Jan, 1 and 8 May, Ascension Day, 14 July, 15 Aug, 1 Nov, and 11 and 25 Dec. In Switzerland (*fêtes générales*): 1 and 2 Jan, Good Friday, Easter Monday, Ascension Day, Whit Monday, 1 Aug (Fête Nationale Suisse), 25 and 26 Dec. In addition, in Switzerland there is the Jeûne Fédéral, an annual religious holiday (*jeûne = fast*) on the third Sunday in September.

Shops, including those for food (but not bars, restaurants or bakeries), will be closed on these occasions.

Changing money It is usually possible to change money in post offices in both countries and there are now many cash machines (*distributeurs de billets de banque*), including in fairly small towns, which accept Visa, cash cards bearing the Cirrus/Maestro logo, and so on. Bank opening hours are similar to those in Britain. Although Switzerland still uses francs, it is usually possible to pay in euros in stations, hotels and youth hostels.

Shops Large **supermarkets** are usually open 'non-stop' (not closing for lunch), Monday to Saturday, in both countries, and often on Sunday mornings in France, although in

Tartes (Section 5)

43

Switzerland they are closed all day Sunday. Otherwise **shops (for food)** in both countries are open until 12pm/12.30pm, and then from 2.30pm/3pm until about 7pm. Those (where they still exist) in small villages are usually shut not only on Sundays but often on Monday mornings (and sometimes afternoons) as well, so considerable organisation is needed, especially in the north of France, if you are not to be caught without supplies when you need them, although **bakeries** and **tabacs/presses** (newsagents) very frequently sell cold drinks and sometimes sandwiches. A **superette** in France is a Spar-type general store found mainly in small places. In Switzerland **petrol stations** frequently include a food shop (but they do not sell any kind of alcoholic drinks).

If you need a regular supply of **hot drinks** you might consider taking a Thermos flask with you. In the section through northern France, for example, although you will pass through plenty of villages, you may not come across a bar or a shop for two days (or more if you hit a weekend or a public holiday). In Switzerland, however, the situation is very much better, and many villages have a café/restaurant where you can get anything from a cup of coffee to, depending on the time of day, a hot meal.

Meals In both France and Switzerland meals are available 12am–2pm and 7–9pm. (Beware that if you are a vegetarian, in France in particular, you will probably eating out very difficult.) Breakfast (in hotels and so on) is usually available from 7am/7.30am onwards.

Cafés and bars In large places these may open as early as 7am, particularly those run by bakeries. Note, however, that restaurants in small places in France often do only hot meals at midday (and only between 12.00am and 1.00pm/1.30pm). And remember, too, that many establishments, in both countries, have a *fermeture hebdomadaire* when they are closed, on a regular basis, on a particular day of the week (these are indicated – 'X Mon', for example – in the text where known).

Post offices These (the PTT in France and La Poste in Switzerland) are open from 8am in large places, 9am in small, until as late as 7pm (12.30pm/1pm on Saturdays), and many of them have cash dispensers too. If you want to send things to yourself further along the route (such as maps and guides) or receive letters, you can do this via the poste restante system whereby you collect your mail (on presentation of your passport) at a particular post office. Letters or parcels should be addressed to yourself (surname first), Poste Restante, followed by the postcode and name of the town. The most likely places you will need are – in France: 62000 Arras, 51100 Reims and 25000 Besançon; in Switzerland – Poste Restante Lausanne, Avenue de la Gare 43b, 1000 Lausanne 01; and Poste Restante Martigny, Avenue de la

Gare 34, 1920 Martigny 1. There is a small fee for each item collected, and they are held for only 15 days before being returned to sender.

Telephones Most public telephones in both France and Switzerland now operate with *télécartes* (phone cards), and there are phone boxes in the centre of almost all villages (and they can take incoming calls as well). All phone numbers in France (the international dialing code is 33) consist of 10 digits, with the prefix 01, 02, 03 04, or 05 at the start of the 8-figure number, according to the region they are in (those beginning with 06 are reserved for mobile phones). In Switzerland (whose international dialing code is 41) telephone numbers also consist of 10 digits, and all mobile phone numbers begin with 07. (Note that if you phone either country from Britain you do not use the '0' in the prefix, in the same way that you omit it when calling Britain from abroad.) The emergency number in France (for all services) is 112. In Switzerland dial 117 for the police, 118 for the fire brigade and 144 for an ambulance.

Mobile phones These are useful for emergencies, but they frequently do not work in rural areas (where there is no *réseau* or coverage), and as there are still plenty of telephone boxes (*cabines téléphoniques*) or *points-phones* along the route, you may consider leaving yours at home. If you do bring your mobile with you it might be better to leave it switched off except for a very limited time each day; you will find it a much more 'pilgrim' journey if your friends and relations back home cannot contact you at all hours.

Internet cafés/cybercafés These are not nearly as easy to find in France as they are in the Swiss section of the route, but as their availability changes frequently they have not been systematically listed in this guide. However, tourist offices can usually tell you where to find one locally.

Launderettes These can be found in all large towns.

Drinking water/fountains There are only a few places along the way in France with a *point d'eau*, either tap or fountain, marked 'eau potable' (safe to drink). There are also many public WCs, particularly in small towns and villages, often in/near the mairie (town hall). All cemeteries in France have water, but you will need to check whether it is safe to drink. In Switzerland, however, there are a lot of public fountains (and public WCs) and if they are not marked 'eau non potable' and are running continuously, the water is usually safe to drink.

Stamps for pilgrim passports. Modern pilgrims who seek to prove their pilgrimage carry pilgrim 'passports' or 'credentials' (*créanciales* in French) which they have stamped (*tamponnée*) at regular intervals along the

45

Clastres Church (Section 3)

way (in churches, tourist offices, town halls, post offices and so on), and which they then present to the authorities in the sacristy in the Vatican when they arrive in Rome to help them obtain their Testimonium (certificate of completion of pilgrimage). More information about pilgrim 'passports' is available (to its members) from the Confraternity of Pilgrims to Rome (see Appendix B).

Churches Although many churches in France are open all day, particularly artistically significant ones and cathedrals, in small towns and villages mass is usually held only once a fortnight – or once a month in really small places. A list of mass times, and where they will be held in the local area, is normally posted in churches for the current and following month. In Switzerland, which has both Roman Catholic and Protestant (Eglise Reformée) churches, the Catholic churches are sometimes open, but the Protestant temples (with the exception of the cathedral in Lausanne) are normally shut except at service times. (Note that the word *église*, in both France and Switzerland, refers to a Catholic church, and *temple* to a Protestant one – you will see this reflected in street names, for example.)

The Reformed church in Switzerland is not a national body, like the Anglican church in England and Wales, for example, but is organized on a cantonal basis, with those in the German part of the country mainly Zwinglian in tradition, and those in the French-speaking areas more Calvinist in background. Since 1920 the Fédération des Eglises Protestantes en Suisse has served as an umbrella organization to deal with relations with the federal government.

For pilgrims who attend mass and would like to be able to join in at least once during the service, the Lord's Prayer is given below in French.

Notre Père qui es aux cieux,
que ton nom soit sanctifié,
que ton règne vienne,
que ta volonté soit faite
sur la terre comme au ciel.
Donne-nous aujourd'hui
notre pain de ce jour.
Pardonne-nous nos offenses,
comme nous pardonnons aussi
à ceux qui nous ont offensés.
Et ne nous soumets pas à la tentation,
mais délivre-nous du Mal.

Medical assistance Travellers from Britain should make sure that they obtain an EHIC (European Health Insurance Card) before setting out (forms are available from the post office). This is a Europe-wide document entitling you to free or reduced medical (but not dental) treatment. (If you already have one, check its expiry date before departure.) Note, however, that the EHIC does not cover transport home, for which you will need separate insurance. If you wear glasses it is advisable to take either a spare pair or the prescription with you.

Above *Via Francigena waymarking on the North Downs Way (Section 1) (photo: William Pettit)*

Right *Tourisme pédestre (TP) signposting in Martigny Croix (Section 6)*

USING THIS GUIDE

Waymarking

Dogs In France dog owners nearly always tell you 'He won't hurt you' ('Il n'est pas méchant'), although this is often hard to believe. They are usually (although not always) tied up, hear you ages before you have any idea where they are and are often enormous (although the small ones are, in fact, a greater nuisance, as they have a nasty habit of letting you pass quietly by and then attacking from behind, nipping you in the back of your ankles). A stick is very useful – not to hit them with, but to threaten. Be warned!

In Switzerland, on the contrary, dogs appear to be extremely well behaved (their owners are obliged to take them to training classes) and are not, in general, a problem.

The route described in this book follows, in the main, the one proposed by the AIVF in their pioneering *Vademecum* in 1994, just after the Via Francigena was declared a European Cultural Itinerary by the Council of Europe. From Canterbury to Dover it follows the North Downs Way, well waymarked not only with that logo but also, now, as the Via Francigena. Once you have crossed the Channel, however, the route is not waymarked at all, except in a few places as you get further southeast before and after Besançon and when the route coincides, for very short sections, with one of the French GR (Grande Randonnée) routes with their red and white *balisage* (waymarking).

There are plans afoot to start systematic signage of the Via Francigena, beginning in the département of the Pas-de-Calais and eventually covering the whole of the route through France, but this has not yet started, so the route described in this book has been chosen to be as direct as possible while remaining both safe and quiet. It is on tracks and footpaths wherever possible, but at other times on minor roads with little traffic and within reasonable access of overnight accommodation. The author of this guide is also very conscious that the vast majority of pilgrims are not experienced walkers, and so need to take clear, recognizable paths that can be used in all weather conditions and by people who are not necessarily very agile. The reader may find that since the preparation of this guide some or all of the signage has been put in place and that it differs, at times, from some of the route-finding information given here, although all reasonable efforts have been made to make this guide as up-to-date and accurate as possible.

Note that in the areas (in France) where the route has been waymarked, and also, to some extent, in Switzerland, this has often been done by local associations walking the Via Francigena in sections, on days out, without necessarily seeing it in the context of the whole route. This has resulted in the waymarking of a series of disjointed outings with a common theme rather than a very long, single pilgrim road leading from Canterbury to Rome.

Since the route is, in the main, not waymarked in France you will, as well as following the instructions in this book, need to equip yourself with maps (see below) in order to find your way. In Switzerland, however, the course of the Via Francigena is now adequately waymarked (in both directions) as their TP (*tourisme pédestre*) route number 70. This takes the form of yellow fingerposts with 'TP' or 'Tourisme pédestre' on them, frequently indicating the altitude of the location and, increasingly, a pilgrim figure or a Via Francigena sticker. In between there are yellow 'lozenges' (horizontal diamonds) with black borders painted on rocks, trees, and so on to remind (and reassure) you that you are still on the right route. (Those continuing their journey into Italy will find that, in general, the route is well waymarked all the way to Rome.)

The Swiss fingerposts frequently have the names of the next places they go to, but rather than indicating distances in kilometres, timings are given instead, something people not used to them often find disconcerting, as you have no conception, unless you already know the area, of how far away the place concerned actually is. Many timings seem optimistic – probably calculated by very tall, very fit walkers out with only a small day sack, rather than by tired pilgrims walking all the way from Canterbury to Rome in one go with a big rucksack, and possibly a tent as well, on their backs. You may find, however, that after a while you can gauge how the timings given coincide (or not) with your own progress.

Be prepared to find that although the route described in this guide follows, for the most part, the VF signage in Switzerland, there are some places where the author has 'straightened out' the intinerary a little so as not to make unnecessary detours. In such cases this is indicated in the text so that readers can, if they wish, follow the VF waymarking instead of the instructions given here for the short sections where the two diverge. There may be other sections, too, where the waymarking has been altered since the preparation of this guide, something that the author has tried to anticipate but cannot, obviously, take responsibility for.

Maps

For such a long route in a guide of this size it is not possible to include detailed digital mapping and, as always in Cicerone guidebooks, carrying copies of printed maps is recommended. The appropriate ones are listed below. (To save weight, you could consider posting each map home as it is finished with, and posting maps for later sections on ahead poste restante for collection at the relevant points. See 'Post office' under 'Other practical information' above.) Sketch maps of the route are provided throughout, for planning purposes, at 1:200,000.

Britain The route from Canterbury to Dover, along the North Downs Way, is covered by two Ordnance Survey maps in the Explorer (1:25,000, 4cm to 1km) series:

- 150 Canterbury and the Isle of Thanet
- 138 Dover, Folkstone and Hythe.

France Michelin 724 is a single map covering the whole of northern France, but the very good maps in the IGN (Institut Géographique National, the equivalent of the Ordnance survey maps in Britain) new lime-green Top 100 Tourisme et Découverte series are recommended for walkers. The scale is 1:100,000 (1cm to 1km), they are GPS compatible and seven are required, listed here in route order:

- 101 Lille – Boulogne-sur-Mer
- 102 Lille – Maubeuge
- 104 Reims – Saint-Quentin
- 110 Reims – Saint-Dizier
- 120 Saint-Dizier – Chaumont
- 130 Vesoul – Langres
- 137 Besançon – Montbéliard.

Switzerland The Swiss publishing firm Kummerley Frey (www.swisstravel center.ch) has a Cartes de Randonnée series (1:60,000, 3km to 5cm), GPS compatible, and the following four cover the course of the Via Francigena from the French border to the Great St Bernard Pass:

Track after Fontaine (Section 4)

- 8 Neuchâtel (Sainte-Croix – Rances – Yverdon-les-Bains)
- 15 Lausanne/Valleee de Joug (Lausanne – Cully – Epesses – Rances – Orbe)
- 16 Gruyère (Chexbres – Vevey – Montreux – Aigle)
- 22 Grand Saint-Bernard/Dents du Midi (Villeneuve – Grand Saint-Bernard).

The whole country is also covered by Swiss Topo maps at various scales. All these maps are available from Stanfords map shop in London, from The Map Shop, Upton-upon-Severn (see Appendix B for addresses) and from many large general bookshops, but make sure you get the latest edition.

Route description

The route is divided up into six sections beginning, respectively, in Canterbury, Calais, Arras, Reims, Besançon and Lausanne – these are all places where walking pilgrims can reach or leave the route easily by public transport, if they need to complete the journey in shorter stages.

Each of the main places along the route appears in a box, with its name in bold, preceded by the distance walked from the previous place. The box also contains a description of the facilities available there, a brief history, where applicable, and an indication of the places of interest to visit. The figures in parentheses after each place name indicate both the distance in kilometres from Canterbury and the distance to the Great St Bernard Pass (in the case of large towns such as Reims the distances are to/from their centres, normally at the cathedral). In addition, where known, the population is given and the altitude in metres above sea level.

The text is deliberately not divided up into daily stages, as in this way the walker can decide the distances he or she would like to cover each day. (It is suggested that you go through the text in advance and mark in possible overnight stops with a highlighter pen.) Key place names appear in the text in **bold type**, as do other names that help in wayfinding, such as street names, the names of prominent buildings, rivers and so on.

Unlike pilgrimages to Lourdes, Fatima or other locations where miracles are sought and help for specific problems requested, and where being in the pilgrim destination itself is the most important factor, on the Via Francigena, like the Camino de Santiago, it is the journey itself that is the pilgrim's principal concern, the arrival in Rome being only a conclusion to the rest of the undertaking. Timings have not been given from place to place, but 4km per hour, exclusive of stops and except in very hilly places, is often considered average, especially when carrying a heavy rucksack. However, a comfortable pace may often be more than this – a fit walker may well be able to maintain a speed of 5–6km or 3½ miles per hour.

By now, hopefully, you will be as prepared as you can be for such a long, challenging undertaking, and ready to follow in the footsteps of the hundreds and thousands of other pilgrims who walked the route in centuries gone by. Putting one foot in front of another, day after day after day, you will (some three months after leaving Canterbury) eventually arrive in the Eternal City – Rome.

Good luck!

CANTERBURY TO DOVER

Christ Church Gate, Canterbury

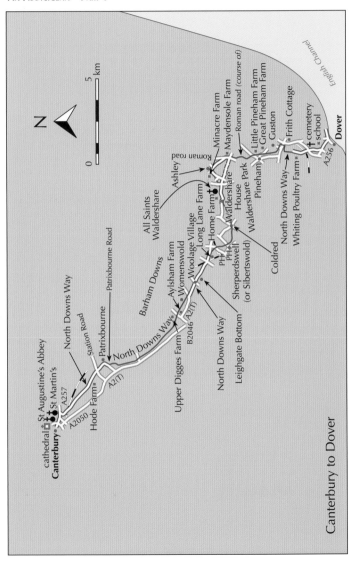

Canterbury to Dover

SECTION 1

Canterbury to Dover (30km)

Canterbury (0/945)

Population 45,000, 42m. Accommodation in all price brackets. YH, 54 New Dover Road, Canterbury, CT1 3DT (0845 371 9010) (K). Kipps Independent Hostel, 40 Nunnery Fields, CT1 3JT (01227 786121) (K). Camping & Caravan Club campsite on Bekesbourne Lane (01227 463216), all year. Canterbury Information Centre, The Buttermarket, 12–13 Sun Street (01227 378100, canterburyinformation@canterbury.gov.uk), has lists of B&Bs, guesthouses, etc. Basic pilgrim accommodation available in Cathedral House, but phone ahead on 01227 762862.

Pilgrim blessings are available in the cathedral if desired (ask in the Welcome Office, where you can also obtain a PS). Official guided walks of Canterbury are available from TO daily. Most of the town's main sights involve an admission fee.

A pilgrim destination in its own right (the word 'canter' is short for 'Canterbury pace' or 'Canterbury gallop', from the supposed easy pace of medieval pilgrims to Canterbury), the town is on the site of an Iron Age settlement, rebuilt by the Romans in AD43. The cathedral was founded in AD597 by Saint Augustine, and has services several times a day, as well as a Romanesque crypt, a 12th-century quire, 12th- and 13th-century stained

glass, including a depiction of a pilgrim on his way to Canterbury in the west window, and the shrine of Thomas à Becket, martyred in the cathedral on 29 Dec 1170. Eastbridge Hospital of Saint Thomas the Martyr (25 High Street) was founded in the 12th century to offer overnight accommodation to poor pilgrims come to visit the shrine of Thomas à Becket and still has the original 12th-century ceiling (an inverted hull, built by shipwrights); today it provides housing for the elderly and has two chapels, a dining hall and a 13th-century painting of Christ in glory, all restored. Greyfriars, built in 1297 and spanning the River Stour (off Stour Street), is the sole remains of Greyfriars Priory, the first Franciscan settlement in Britain and its oldest remaining Franciscan building. It contains a chapel (communion service Wed 12.30pm). Admission free.

Saint Martin's Church (North Holmes Road) is the oldest parish church in England still in continuous use. Saint Augustine came to worship here before he established a monastery of his own. It was originally a Roman building, but was given by King Ethelbert to his French Christian wife in AD597 for use as a chapel and enlarged. It was later enlarged again in the 12th century and a tower added in the 14th (services Sunday at 9.00am and 6.30pm). Saint Peter's Church (St Peter's Street) is thought to stand on the site of a church built for the local Christian community in Roman times, and perhaps rebuilt by Saint Augustine and his monks in Saxon days. The tower dates from about 1100 and has four bells dating from the 14th to the 17th centuries. Saint Dunstan's Church (St Dunstan's Street) is over 1000 years old and the first to be dedicated to this saint, who was Archbishop of Canterbury from AD960 to 978. Saint Augustine's Abbey (Longport) was founded by Saint Augustine in AD598, and is where the saint and his convert King Ethelbert are buried.

Other places of interest include the ruins of the Norman Canterbury Castle (admission free), West Gate Towers (St Peter's Street) – a medieval fortified gatehouse, the Canterbury Tales visitor attraction (St Margaret's Street), the Museum of Canterbury (Stour Street), the Roman Museum (Butchery Lane), and the Royal Museum and Art Gallery (admission free).

The route from Canterbury to Dover on the Via Francigena follows the North Downs Way, which also coincides in part with the Elham Valley Way, both long-distance footpaths and waymarked in both directions. Note, however, that apart from the shop and pubs in Shepherdswell (Sibertswold, 16.5km) there is nowhere to eat or drink between Canterbury and Dover, so go prepared.

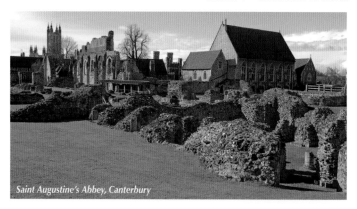

Saint Augustine's Abbey, Canterbury

From the cathedral, and with your back to the main entrance, go through the gateway opposite (**Christ Church Gate**) and turn L down **Burgate**. Cross the ring road at the end and KSO ahead down **Church Street**, passing **Saint Paul's Church** (on R). Turn R into **Monastery Street** and then immediately L into **Longport** (not marked at the start), passing the ruins of **Saint Augustine's Abbey** (on L). (**Note** If you stay in the YH you can turn L out of its gate onto **New Dover Road** and then R into **St Augustine's Road**, which runs into the **Pilgrims Way** at the end.)

KSO ahead at roundabout, passing the prison (on L). *(To visit Saint Martin's Church turn L up North Holmes Road and then retrace your steps afterwards.)*

Turn R at next junction into **Spring Lane**, then 100m later turn R again into **Pilgrims Way**. Turn L 100m after that by houses onto tarmac FP. Continue along it *(note Pilgrims Lodge on R, 'retirement home for ladies and gentlemen')* to T-junction, then turn R over railway line through estate of modern houses (still called **Pilgrims Way**). At the end KSO ahead on tarred lane with tall hedges to either side, after which you come out into open country. When you reach a fork with a more major path leading R, KSO(L) ahead here (to L of hedge).

KSO, quite literally, ignoring turns to L and R, for 2.5km, until a minor road joins from back R, just before a small roundabout on the outskirts of

5km Patrixbourne (5/940)

Small village with Saint Mary's Norman church (Swiss stained-glass windows).

Patrixbourne church

KSO through village, following road round, veering R past church then, after last house, fork L off road onto FP diagonally across field towards woods. Turn R there to follow FP along edge of woods towards A2 (*nice views and handy seat part-way along*).

At end turn L through small gate onto shady FP parallel to the A2, that you can't see but can (very definitely!) hear below you to R. Reach a road bridge 500m later and KSO ahead on other side. 150m later fork L across fields to some woods, then continue with them on your LH side. Continue ahead through fields for 3km (this area is Barham Downs), crossing three minor tarred roads until your reach a house on your R and then another on your L (**Upper Digge Farm**). Do **not** KSO ahead here on the more obvious track in front of you, but turn L then fork R immediately past a building. Turn R onto a farm track and KSO, ignoring turns until you reach the B2406, by a cemetery on your R. (*The North Downs Way does, in fact, cut across the top corner of the last field on your L, but you may miss it if it has been ploughed up recently.*)

Turn L (if necessary) and then turn R 100m later (or cross over, as applicable) onto grassy track following line of telegraph poles. KSO(L) at junction of paths to road in small village of

6.5km Womenswold (11.5/933.5)

Saint Margaret's Church (to R, seat in churchyard; info about keyholders in porch).

To continue, turn L at road then immediately R (staggered junction) to R of wall then to L of hedge and reach minor road. Cross over, go through woods and then turn R onto another minor road at entrance to **Woolage Village**. Here the North Downs Way turns L over a stile alongside the village green and then R at the end to a road, but you can cut across the green diagonally (*seats and picnic tables*) and then turn L onto a minor road. The FP then continues to its left in a field, before returning to it shortly before a sharp LH bend. KSO(R) here, up a tunnel-like shady FP.

1.5km later reach a minor road at bend by bridge over railway line. Turn L over it then R down **Long Lane** (minor road) downhill on other side. Pass **Long Lane Farm** and 150m later turn R onto grassy lane and go through field to junction of two minor roads. Turn R, cross railway line (*this is North Bank Crossing, on East Kent Railway, open weekends*) ▼, then turn L through sm all field (seat, picnic table). KSO ahead at end, by houses, up shady lane. Go uphill through two

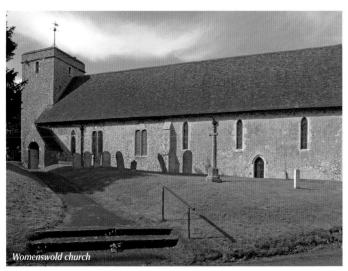

Womenswold church

fields, alongside a third on a lane, cross cycle track and continue on lane between houses to emerge on road in Shepherdswell.

If you want to visit the shop directly KSO ahead on road after crossing the railway line to a road junction with the Co-op and the Bricklayers Arms pub (does food). Then turn L up Church Hill to the Bell Inn on the village green near the church. Turn L here to continue on the North Downs Way.

5km Shepherdswell (or Sibertswold) (16.5/928.5)

Bell Inn (does food), Co-op on road – go down Church Lane to RH side of pub. Village green to R, with Saint Andrew's Church (Norman/Romanesque).

Turn R on road then immediately L on FP alongside cemetery. Go along edges of two fields, across the middle of two more, through some woods, along one more field then turn L into next one along its edge. Cross next field diagonally to top RH corner and reach minor road. Turn R to crossroads at edge of **Coldred** (*a village, 1.5km, B&B at Colret House, The Green, 01304 830388*), then fork L at opposite corner (between **Coldred Road** and **Singledge Lane**) on FP through woods. Cross a field, go through some more woods and then cross a very large field towards edge of **Waldershare Park** (woods). Go over stile, cross field diagonally L (ie continuing your previous line of travel), cross next field diagonally as well, and cross drive and then stile in LH corner by

3km Waldershare House (19.5/925.5)

Elegant Palladian mansion, set in a large park.

Veer L then R, passing through white gate, veering L between fenced-in fields to junction. *This is Hornby's Fields, named after Mary Hornby, whose legacy enabled the planting of 1237 saplings to replace the trees lost in the Great Storm of 1987.* Turn R here, but then fork L immediately over stile into field,▼ cross it diagonally to **Pidders Wood**, a circular enclosure of trees, and out again on the other side and into the churchyard of **All Saints Waldershare**. The church is no longer in use, but is open daily 10.30am–3.30pm. Go past church, out through the lych gate (seats under cover), continue to road and turn R past it to junction opposite lodge to **Waldershare House**. Turn L here to cross road bridge over the A256.

However, if there are bulls in this field KSO ahead up lane to its RH side, reach road by the lodge and cross it in order to then cross the road bridge over the A256.

50m later ▼ turn L down a concrete drive towards **Minacre Farm**, but 100m before house fork R over stile, continuing diagonally towards drive, then fork L over another stile, continue diagonally towards woods and reach minor road. Turn L along it, following road round to R, in **Ashley** (2km).

The official route does a 'kink' here, but if you are short of time, or in bad weather, you can KSO on road here, KSO(R) at bend (marked 'West Langdon') for 1.5km to the junction by Maydensole Farm, and then turn R on minor road (marked 'Whitfield, Dover') to continue.

When road bends sharp L KSO ahead on lane (**Northdowns Close**) and KSO ahead between hedges, slightly downhill, and then between fields. Cross another field, reach a road coming at an angle from back L, turn R along it and reach crossroads by

3km Maydensole Farm (22.5/922.5)

From here you follow the course of the old Roman road, in a straight line (almost literally) all the way into Dover.

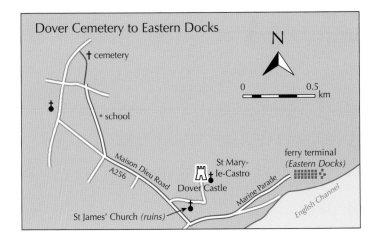

Dover Cemetery to Eastern Docks

Dover docks, looking across the Channel to Cap Gris Nez and Wissant

KSO ahead at crossroads then KSO(L) ahead when lane bends R, up tunnel-like lane to start with, opening out between fields. KSO 1.5km later, reach minor road, turn R along it then fork L immediately up sunken lane. Emerge on road by T-junction 500m later. Follow road round to R and then L, past farm in **Pineham**. Turn R up grassy lane uphill.

KSO for nearly 1km until you reach the A2, then turn L alongside it on small FP below road for 500m until you go up a slope to a road. Turn R over bridge, then turn R on other side along another small FP to LH side of road. 300m later reach metal field gate and fork L across field to woods. Turn R along FP side, continue to a T-junction of similar paths and then turn L.

KSO (literally), the path becoming sunken lane after a while. 500m later another FP joins from back R by house and path becomes old tarred lane (Roman road), descending to junction by main entrance gates to **Charlton cemetery** on the outskirts of Dover. Cross over and turn R down **Old Charlton Road**. After junction with gates to **Connaught Park** turn second L into **Castle Avenue** then fork R down **Park Avenue** to junction with **Charlton Green**. Turn L here along **Maison Dieu Road**, after which the North Downs Way turns R into **Pencester Road** to go to the centre of Dover. However, if you want to go straight to the ferry terminal KSO here to the end of **Maison Dieu Road**, continue on **Woolcomber Street**, passing ruins of **Saint James's Church** (on L), and then turn L at the traffic lights along **Marine Parade** to the **Eastern Docks**.

7.5km Dover (30/915) Pop. 35,000

Accommodation in all price brackets. YH now closed. East Cliff Hotel, 28 East Cliff/Marine Parade (01304 202299), near ferry terminal, reported to be pilgrim friendly. No campsite. TO in Old Town Gaol, Biggin (01304 205108, tic@doveruk.com).

Trains to London Victoria. National Express coaches (shuttle service to London Victoria Coach Station, to/from both the Pencester Road bus stand and the Eastern Ferry Terminal).

P&O ferries for Calais leave every 45mins from the terminal in the Eastern Docks, where the port service bus takes you to the ferry.

Dover's most prominent sight is its castle, built in the 12th century on the site of an Iron Age fort at the top of the famous white cliffs. Its main feature is its secret wartime tunnels, built originally in the 12th century and adapted during the Napoleonic Wars, and its underground hospital. Above ground there is the Roman lighthouse and the Saxon church of Saint Mary-de-Castro, dating back to AD1000. Expensive admission fee, but worth it if you have plenty of time to visit.

The Roman Painted House (New Street) is a well-preserved Roman *mansio* (official hotel) with intact wall paintings, hypocaust and the remains of Roman fort walls and bastion.

Dover's other sights include the Maison Dieu, now the town hall but formerly a hospital, dating from the 13th century, Saint Edmund's Chapel, Saint Mary's Church and the remains of a Benedictine priory.

The English Channel is 34km (21 miles) wide between Dover and Calais, and the ferry crossing normally takes 1½hrs. (Note that in calculating running totals of distances between Canterbury and the Great Saint Bernard Pass, the Channel crossing is not included!)

CALAIS TO ARRAS

Arras town hall

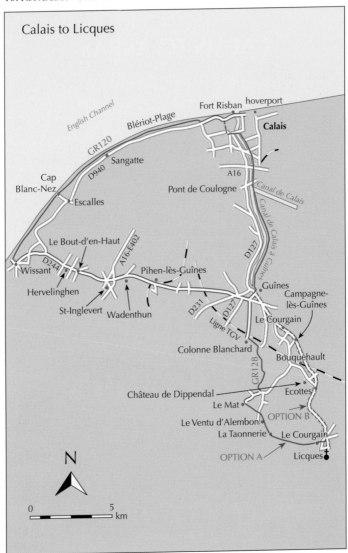

SECTION 2
Calais to Arras (124km)

Calais (30/915)

Pop. 80,000. Town with all facilities. Accommodation in all price brackets. YH (also known as Centre Européen de Séjour, CIS), Avenue du Maréchal de Lattre de Tassigny (03.21.34.70.20, adjcalais@wanadoo.fr). **Camping municipal, Avenue Raymond Poincaré (near sea, all year, 03.21.97.89.79). TO: Boulevard Georges Clemenceau 12 (near railway station, 03.21.96.62.40, ot@ot-calais.fr). Plenty of hotels (check in TO). Internet in Cyber-Phone, Rue du Duc de Guise 42.

Red-brick hôtel de ville (1925), in neo-Flemish style, with Rodin's sculpture group 'Les Bourgeois de Calais' ('The Burghers of Calais', 1895) in the garden in front; Eglise Notre-Dame; Tour de Guet (watch tower); and old town (an island); Bastions de la Citadelle 1560; Musée des Beaux Arts et et la Dentelle (25 Rue Richelieu – lace centre, worth a visit if you are interested in this). Blériot, the French aviator who made the first air crossing of the English Channel, took off from just outside Calais.

As you come into Calais on the ferry you can see the GR120 (on the route via Wissant) to your R – along the promenade and then on the beach to the west.

Hôtel de Ville

When you come out of the ferry terminal building, by the bus stop for journeys into the city centre, turn R and go up a ramp (marked 'Piétons') that doubles back on itself. It then turns L and then R along a walkway before bringing you down to the street just before a roundabout. KSO ahead here (**Avenue Jacques Cousteau**, signposted 'Centre Ville'), veering L to go over the **Pont Vetillard**. Continue ahead on **Rue Lamy** to the **Place de Suède**.

The historic route, the one taken by Sigeric and waymarked spasmodically with the red and white balises (waymarks) of the French GR (long-distance footpath) network, went via Wissant, 21km to the west of Calais, which at that time was the port for arrival/departure from Britain and the shortest channel crossing point. Today you can go there either along the coast road (D940, fairly quiet and with good views) or by taking the GR120, a long-distance footpath along the beach, much of it on loose sand (very tiring to walk on), via Sangatte and Cap Blanc Nez. Wissant is only a small town nowadays with 1100 inhabitants in winter (half the town was submerged in a sandstorm in 1738 and again in 1777, after which it fell into disuse as a cross-channel port). SCR, TO (03.21.85.39.64), PO, pharmacie, 4 hotels, **camping municipal (info. from cotedopale@wanadoo.fr). From here you then turn hard left (to form a narrow isosceles triangle), east again, to Guînes (15km more, 36km in all by this route, but only 12km south of Calais!), on minor roads and passing through Hervelingen (***Camping La Vallée), Saint-Inglevert, Wadenthun and Pihen-lès-Guînes.

'Les Bourgeois de Calais' by Auguste Rodin, hôtel de ville, Calais

'Towpath in reverse' sign, Canal de Guînes

For the **historic route** (or to visit Calais) turn R out of the **Place de Suède** into the **Rue du Commandant Bonnique** and continue on the **Rue de Thermes** to the **Place d'Armes**. Turn R there into **Rue de la Mer**, cross the bridge and at the roundabout fork L up **Avenue Raymond Poincaré** (YH to L on **Avenue Maréchal de Lattre de Tassigny**, campsite signposted to R). For the **GR120 and Wissant** continue ahead to the seashore and then veer L past the **Poste de Sécurité** along the promenade (**Digue Gaston Berthe**).

The historic route is not described in its entirety this guide, however – it is a very long way to Rome, and you may not want to make detours, especially near the start of your journey. A short-cut is suggested instead, via the Canal de Calais, direct to Guînes. This route is flat, although it is on tarmac for the first 3km, as far as the Pont de Coulogne. There are a few bars/cafés along the way on the LH bank, but the RH side of the canal has less traffic.

Short-cut From the **Place d'Armes** in the centre of Calais (2km from the port) turn L into **Rue Royale**, continue on **Boulevard Clemenceau**, cross bridge over **Bassin de la Marne**, pass railway station (R) and KSO to junction with **Avenue Président Wilson** and **Rue Paul Bert** (public park opposite to R). Cross diagonally L here in front of the hôtel de ville (*note Rodin's group sculpture 'The Burghers of Calais' to R*), then turn L into **Rue Jean Jaurès**. Turn R at end onto **Quai du Commerce** and go along the **Canal de Calais**.

(However, if you want to continue directly to Guînes without visiting Calais, from the **Place de Suède**, KSO ahead on other side of square down the **Rue de Londres** to the **Place d'Angleterre**, and then KSO(L) ahead down the **Rue de Hollande** to the **Place de Norvège**. Cross the bridge over the **Bassin de la Batellerie**, continue to the junction with the **Rue Mollien** and turn R onto the **Canal de Calais**.)

KSO for 2.5km until you reach the road bridge at the

5km Pont de Coulogne (35/910)

Cafés.

Continue on the RH bank of the canal on the **Chemin de Contre Halage** (ie 'towpath on the other side' or 'towpath in reverse'). 500m later the canal divides into two, the **Canal de Calais à Guînes** (which you will take) forking R (west). Go up slope to cross bridge over the branch canal then on other side turn L down some steps and L again to go under a pedestrian bridge under the railway. You are now on the LH bank and at the start of the **Chemin de Randonnée Pedestre de Coulogne à Guînes**, a reasonably well-waymarked path on grassy lanes.

40–50m later turn L onto a very minor tarmac road, veering R, and then fork L off it opposite an isolated garage by a stile (railway line is now on your L) onto a grassy lane to L of tarmac lane (**Avenue des Lys**). KSO. 2km later cross a tarmac road near the **Ecluse Carrée** (a lock) and continue ahead over FB over dyke down similar lane. Cross unsurfaced road then KSO, parallel to private drive to L. Pass small farm and watch out carefully as the FP is waymarked but it is difficult to see. After that, the path continues close to the canal. 500m later it becomes an unsurfaced road that reaches the D248E1 on the outskirts of **Marais de Guînes** (*Ecomusée Saint-Joseph Village, museum of village life*).

However, if you want to go to **La Belle Pêche campsite (Route de Guînes, 03.21.35.21.07, 01/05–31/10, resto) turn R here over the canal and then L along the D217–you will have to continue on that the following mornng as there are no more bridges until you reach Guînes.

Here the **Chemin de Randonnée** continues on the other side of the road, but turn R instead and then L to walk along the towpath to Guînes (3km, despite the signpost telling you it is '5km, 1h30'). Reach the end of the canal (junction with river to L) at the entrance to the town. The main road veers L, but KSO ahead on **Rue Maréchal Joffre** (marked 'Centre Ville'), veering L. Turn R into **Rue Massenet** and reach **Place Foch** with the hôtel de ville in the centre of

7km Guînes (42/903) Pop. 5000, 6m

SCR, Pharmacie, TO (03.21.35.73.73), PO, Camping ***La Bien Assise (on D231, from Wissant, 03.21.35.20.77, 10/04–24/09) has pilgrim-only accommodation in small hut, 4 places, communal facilities. (To get there, from the square in front of the hôtel de ville KSO ahead on Rue de Guizelin to junction with Boulevard Delannoy (L) and Avenue de la Libération (R) and turn R here.) CH La Forge, Rue Guizelin 32 (03.21.34.70.14). Hotel L'Auberge du Colombier on D231 next to campsite (03.21.36.93.00).

Tour de l'Horloge (theme park, Rue du Château) on the site of the Drap d'Or (Field of the Cloth of Gold), where Henry VIII had his famous encounter with the French king François I. Church of Saint-Pierre.

Guînes was stage LXXVIII (Gisne, 78) in Sigeric's itinerary (it was compiled on his return journey though, so the first stage started in Rome); stage LXXX (Sumeran, 80) is Sombre (3km from Wissant, inland), but LXXIX (79) is missing (unless, as has been suggested, the author of Sigeric's itinerary miscounted…).

From Guînes to Licques you have two options – one via part of the GR128 (15km), the other, more direct, on the road (10.5km, recommended for bikes).

OPTION A – GR128 ROUTE

From **Place Foch** continue ahead on **Rue Clemenceau** then turn L by pond into **Rue du Bassin**. Turn R at end into **Boulevard Blanchard** and at end cross D231. KSO(L) ahead, slightly staggered on the **Chemin du Bois de Guînes** (not marked at start but signposted 'Colonne Blanchard'), which then becomes **Chemin du**

Colonne Blanchard, Forêt de Guînes

Ballon, rising gently all the time. 3km from Guînes cross TGV track and 250m later reach woods at a clearing with notice board, seats, and turn L here onto a sandy track, the GR128 (not waymarked at start). *The Colonne Blanchard is uphill to R in woods, a monument erected in honour of the aeronauts Jean-Pierre Blanchard and the American Dr Jeffries who landed here after the first successful balloon crossing of the English Channel in 1785. The journey, in a gas balloon, started in Dover and took 1¾hrs to accomplish.*

The GR128 is marked with signposts, but for most of the way to Licques they only indicate the route in the reverse direction, so watch out carefully at junctions.

Turn R at T-junction of similar tracks, then turn L 500m later at T-junction of similar tracks. *The route is also waymarked, in red, for the 'Sentier de l'Epinette' and, in yellow, for 'Entre les Bois', two local routes that coincide for much of the way to Licques with the GR128.* 350m later reach a very minor road. Cross over then fork (not turn) R on other side, '1 o'clock' style (not signposted), then turn L at crossing of similar tracks 500m later (also not signposted). 1km later turn R by marker post 71 (marked with yellow 'Entre les Bois' signpost) onto narrower, shady path, rising gently all the time. KSO for nearly 2km, coming partly out of the woods halfway along, and then reach wider track coming from R at right angles. Turn L here (the two paths to L join up shortly afterwards). Reach edge of woods, go through a red and white barrier under HT cables and continue on track between fields to a minor road.

Here the GR128 does a detour to west (presumably to visit the gîte de groupe at Le Mât), before returning east, round two sides of a triangle (2.5km), all of it on tarmac. However, it is suggested that you turn L (east) instead when you come out of the woods and reach the minor road and then, when you reach the D248, turn R and continue on it for 2km to the junction with the D191. KSO here (marked 'Licques'), veering L into **Le Ventu d'Alembon** (a hamlet), then turn L in the middle of it down the **Chemin de Sanghen**, signposted 'La Taonnerie'. KSO then follow road as it bends R. Tarmac becomes a gravel track after houses end, veering L along ridge with splendid views on a clear day.

KSO along this track for nearly 3km, ignoring turns to R and L and passing junction with other GRs, one of which suggests an alternative 4km (ie longer) option for going to Licques. When track eventually begins to descend, keep close to hedge to R, descending all the time. At the bottom another track (a GR) joins from back R. KSO ahead until you reach a minor road, where you can either turn R to reach road and then turn L along it to abbey/church in Licques or, alternatively, KSO ahead, reach D215 and then turn R along it to junction near abbey (café) and then turn L for 'Licques Centre'.

OPTION B – ROAD ROUTE

From **Place Foch** and the hôtel de ville in Guînes go back down **Rue Massenet** then turn R into **Rue Sidney Bowin**, continue to end (staggered), cross **Boulevard Blanchard** and KSO along Boulevard Boulanger and then the **Avenue du Camp du Drap d'Or**. Cross over the D231, then KSO on D215 for 1.5km to junction with D248, a more minor road. Fork R along it into the centre of

4km Campagne-lès-Guînes
Café.

Continue ahead on the D248, passing under the London–Paris (Eurostar) line to

1.5km Bouquehault
Restaurant (X Mon).

When you have passed the church turn L here (*mairie* opposite, resto to your L) onto **Rue de l'Ecole**, a more minor road, marked 'C, Rodelinghem, Ecottes'. At unmarked crossroads 500m later KSO uphill towards woods, passing entrance to **Château Dippendal**. 1km later reach D215 again on outskirts of

1.5km Ecottes

Turn R (a long slog) and KSO, undulating, for 3km to the centre of Licques.

15km (from Guînes) Licques (57/888) Pop. 450, 82m

SCR, pharmacie, 2 campsites, both to L of D191 on leaving town. ***Camping Les Pommiers des Trois Pays, Rue de Breui 253 (03.21.35.02.02), café and meals; pilgrim friendly and has mobile home to rent per night if free (phone ahead). Camping 1/4–31/10, chalets all year. **Le Canchy, Rue de Canchy 830 (03.21.82.63.41), 1km further on, all year, also has brasserie. 2km away, at Audenfort, Hôtel/Resto L'Auberge du Moulin (03.21.00.13.16).

Eglise de la Nativité de Notre Dame, all that remains of the Premonstratensian abbey founded there in 1075. Château (1726).

Both routes If you have come on the GR128 you will arrive at the top of the town by the church (with recently restored organ and loft). KSO ahead here at junction on the D216 marked 'Hocquingheim'. Fork L 1km later to La Claye (3km from Licques), then KSO(L) ahead on the D216E for 3km until you reach the junction with the turning to Fouquesolles. KSO here on the **Rue du Bois de Journy**.

However, if you want to go to one of the campsites, go down hill when you reach the church, marked 'Licques Centre', and turn R at bottom (where those coming along the road route will do so from the L). At junction at top of hill by football ground KSO ahead on the D191, then the following day continue ahead on D191 for 2km, pass the junction at **La Quingoie**, *KSO for 1km more and then turn R at the (staggered) junction with D233 to L marked 'Fouquesolles'. 400m later turn L onto a very minor road (***Rue du Bois de Journy**, *marked 'sauf riverains' – residents only).*

1km later KSO at next (staggered to R) crossing, and 500m later turn L at T-junction with industrial buildings onto **Chemin de la Puiserie** (although not marked until end), veering R to another T-junction (with a wayside cross) at entry to village. Turn R here and KSO for 500m more to junction just past church in centre of

9km Alquines (66/879) Pop. 797, 100m

Bar/shop/bakery (behind church), does meals; 2nd bar. Fort de la Motte, 16th century. (Note that not all, but a lot, of churches in this area are unlocked, even if their doors look shut.)

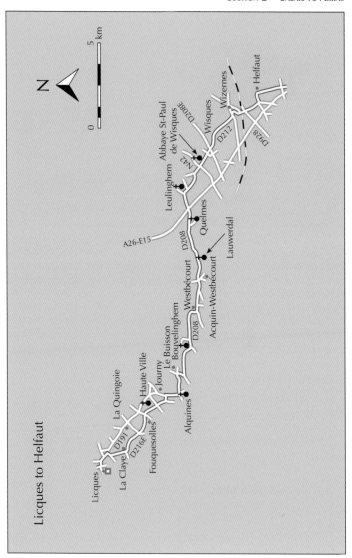

Licques to Helfaut

Countryside near Westbécourt

Turn L at junction and continue on D216 (marked 'Quercamps'), uphill (on **Route du Buisson**) to hamlet of **Le Buisson**, veering R at top. Turn R at junction by bus shelter onto minor road marked 'C, Fromental' (this is the **Rue de Mont Breuchet**), then 400m later turn L along very narrow minor road (unmarked) with wayside cross at junction. This very soon becomes an unsurfaced road, and 200m later veers round to the L (do **not** continue straight ahead here). Follow this road downhill for just over 1km, then turn R at T-junction of similar tracks, uphill via sharp LH bend, to reach the main street and turn L along it in

2km Bouvelinghem (68/877) Pop. 148, 175m

Bar, shop/restaurant to R as you enter village.

Continue past church (on L), downhill, and at junction KSO(R) on D208 for 2km to

2km Westbécourt (70/875)

Follow road round through village, turn L at junction, still on D208, and KSO until you reach the junction with the D225 in

2km Acquin-Westbécourt (72/873) Pop. 625

Café/boulangerie and café-tabac, both near church. CH Mme Deneuville, Rue Principale 49 (on L at junction, 03.21.39.62.57). 13th-century tower and château (cours de ferme) of Prieuré de Saint-Bertin. Church of Sainte-Petronille, 16th–19th centuries, with 15th-century virgin and bell-tower.

Turn L at junction (CH on L), then 100m later turn R uphill on D208 (marked 'Quelmes'). KSO, passing a farm at **Lauwerdal** and a wayside chapel en route until you reach

4.5km Quelmes (76.5/868.5)

A very long, straggling village.

Continue through it and out the other end, still on the D208, cross the bridge over the motorway and 1km later turn R on the D212 into

2.5km Leulinghem (79/866)

Fork L at church along **Rue de l'Ecole** and continue out into open countryside, veering R to a T-junction with another road 1.5km later. Turn R here, cross the N42 and continue past the **Abbaye Saint-Paul** (on your L) into the centre of

2.5km Wisques (82/863) Pop. 146, 126m

Two Benedictine abbeys in this village, both of which can offer accommodation to pilgrims and both have daily monastic offices which you can attend. Saint-Paul (Rue de l'Ecole) is on the L as you enter the village (hot@abbaye-stpaul-wisques.com, 03.21.12.28.55), and the monks put up both male and female visitors. The Abbaye Notre-Dame, Rue de la Fontaine 24 (03.21.95,12.26, ndwisques@wanadoo.fr), is run by nuns and is up on the hill (turn R in the centre of the village). It accommodates female visitors only.

Abbaye de Saint-Paul, Wisques

Continue through the village, cross the D208 (**Hotel/Restaurant La Sapinère (Logis de France) uphill to R, Route Setques 12, 03.21.38.94.00, lasapiniere2@ wanadoo.fr), and KSO ahead on D212 to

3km Wizernes (85/860)
SCRB but no accommodation.

Note There are few shops and hardly any bars en route between here and Arras, so you will need to go supplied with adequate amounts of food and water.
Pass cemetery (on L), reach crossing with D211, turn L (marked 'Centre Ville') and turn R by 36 (**Rue Leo Lagrange**, which becomes **Rue Pierre Mendès-France** (you are on the D198)), veering R to cross river (twice) and railway line. Then take second turning to R (**Rue de Blendeques**) by town exit boards and turn R up **Rue d'Helfaut** (marked 'Thérouanne 8, Inghem 4.5'). This is joined from the back by a bigger road. At the top of the hill, 1km later, turn L on D195 to centre of

1.5km Helfaut (86.5/858.5) Pop. 1731

Shops, cafés, etc. Camping Les Genêts, Rue Parfum des Sapins (03.21.93.80.56). La Coupole, a gigantic concrete bunker, with a concrete dome 5m thick, was built by Hilter in 1943 as a launching base to attack London. Still intact, it is now a museum, the Centre d'Histoire et de Mémoire du Nord – Pas-de-Calais.

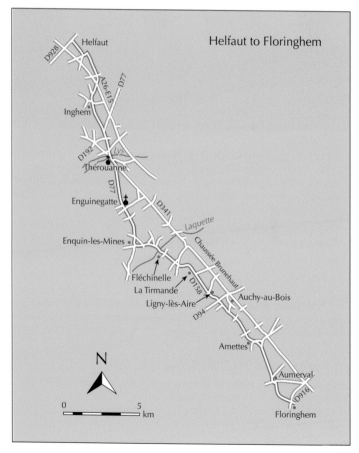

Helfaut to Floringhem

Wayside cross after Helfaut

Turn R by war memorial onto D198 (**Rue de Thérouanne**), passing church (on R). KSO.

200m before crossing motorway note wayside cross hidden in trees to R. Cross bridge over A26 and KSO, passing large brick chapel on R at entry to village, into centre of

4.5km Inghem (91/854) Pop. 313

Bar at junction in centre (does food). Bus shelter opposite.

KSO(L) ahead at junction and continue ahead on D198 until you reach the junction with the D157 (a much larger, busier road). Turn R along it for 200m to a roundabout and then turn second L along the D77 for 1km into

3.5km Thérouanne (94.5/850.5) Pop. 1044, 38m

Shops, banks, etc; bar/resto (X Mon) to R at first junction in town. TO (03.21.93.81.22), with Musée Archéolgique, in centre.

Sigeric's stage LXXVII (Teranburh, 77). Thérouanne, a Roman capital and once one of the richest bishoprics in northern France, with its biggest cathedral, was razed to the ground by Charles V in 1553. Now only quite a small place, the last vestige of the ancient town is the Chapelle de Nielles les Thérouanne, on the banks of the River Lys.

Continue to next junction, in town centre, then turn L along D341 (marked 'Ecques') for 1km (main street, with shops, etc), crossing the **River Lys**. At fork with D157 KSO(R) ahead on D341, marked 'Enguingatte' and 'Enquin-les-Mines'.

This is the start of the Chaussée Brunehaut, a Roman road built to link Arras and Thérouanne with the sea, and so facilitate the Roman invasion of northern France and Belgium. You will follow it most of the way to Arras. It was so named because Queen Brunehaut (the formidable Brunhilde – who met a gruesome death at the age of 80 by being tied to the tail of a galloping horse) had large-scale improvements made to this road in the sixth century.

300m later fork R up Rue de Saint-Pol (D77), uphill. KSO into

5km Enguinegatte (99.5/845.5) Pop. 381, 92m

Continue through village to end, passing small wayside chapel at start, very large modern brick church in centre and another small wayside chapel at end, all on your RH side. KSO ahead again on D77 until you reach

2.5km Enquin-les-Mines (102/843)

A very long, straggling village, with 2 bars at end.

Continue downhill to junction with D158, and then turn L (**Rue des Ecoles**) into centre of village (first bar opposite mairie). At junction after bar turn R into **Rue du Château d'Eau** (marked 'La Flechinelle') and continue to next crossroads (passing another bar, to L), then turn R into **Rue Ernest Hernand** (*note terril – large pointed slag heap – to R, typical of many in this in this formerly very active mining area*). At bottom of hill continue ahead, cross river and then, by bus shelter with seat, turn hard L uphill on **Rue de la Barre**.

KSO. Pass through **Le Transvaal** (hamlet) and KSO. Road then becomes **Rue de la Tirmande**. Reach **La Tirmande** (an extremely long, drawn-out small village – bus shelter with seat in centre) and continue ahead on **Rue de la Cavée**.

After a while the road becomes **Rue de la Tirmande** again, as you have now entered

5.5km Ligny-lès-Aire (107.5/837.5)

KSO through village and at end, where houses become more dense, road veers R and then, at junction, turns L (still the **Rue de la Tirmande**) to church (on L). Turn R here into **Rue de L'Eglise**, following it round to L *(note brick wayside cross at bend)* to junction with very large wayside cross (on R). Continue ahead on **Rue de Rely** and then, 100m later (another brick wayside shrine on L), KSO ahead on D90 (**Rue d'Auchy**). Reach crossing with D94 by large *château d'eau* (water tower).

Here you can turn L for the two CH in **Auchy-au-Bois** (1km off route) – Mme Bulot, Rue de Pernes 28 (03.21.02.09.47) and Mme De-Saint-Laurent-Tailly, Rue Neuve 13 (03.21.25.80.09). *Note that if you sleep here you do not have to retrace your steps, but can return to the route by turning L in the centre of village (marked 'Nedon') and then turning L along Rue d'en Haut (see below) to continue directly to Amettes.*

Otherwise, cross over the D94 and KSO on other side (unmarked). 1km later reach a crossroads with houses and continue on other side (**Rue d'en Haut**, seat). Reach another crossing shortly afterwards, after which the road becomes unsurfaced. KSO for 2km to a T-junction and turn L onto unsurfaced lane, veering R (lane becomes **Rue d'Auchy en Bois**) to T-junction by bus stop (shelter with seat) in

5km Amettes (112.5/832.5)

Bar/bakery, Estaminet Saint-Benoît, Rue de l'Eglise 15 (03.21.26.00.93), Wed–Sat all day, meals, Sun lunch only. *Abri pèlerin* (spartan accommodation) in large hall below Estaminet, in next street (ask about key in bar/bakery). Picnic tables (shady) by mairie. CH Mme Gevas, Rue de l'Eglise 2 (03.21.27.15.02). Accommodation possible with the sisters in the Communauté des Augustines, Rue de l'Eglise 12 (03.21.27.48.78, who run the old people's home next door and are often full with church groups), but only when Mme Gevas is fully booked.

Birthplace of Saint-Benoît Labry, one of the patron saints of pilgrims, who died in poverty on the steps of a church in Rome in 1783 (his house can be visited). Eglise Saint-Sulpice, chapel, with stations of the cross.

Birthplace of Saint-Benoît Labre, Amettes

Turn L and then almost immediately R, between houses 18 and 20, going uphill past the **Maison de Saint-Benoît** and chapel up to church. Turn L there, veering R past it, downhill to junction with large wayside cross. Fork R to unsurfaced road and KSO, ignoring RH turn after 1km, until you reach the D91. Turn R along it into

2.5km Aumerval (115/830)

At begining of village, opposite area with bus shelter, turn hard L into **Rue de Floringhem**. 400m later, at crossing with small wayside chapel on L, turn R and continue on minor road between fields, veering L by house and junction with track at **Moulin des Evits** (bench). Road then becomes **Rue d'Aumerval**. Continue to junction with D916 in

2km Floringhem (117/828)
Bar at crossing (but not always open?).

83

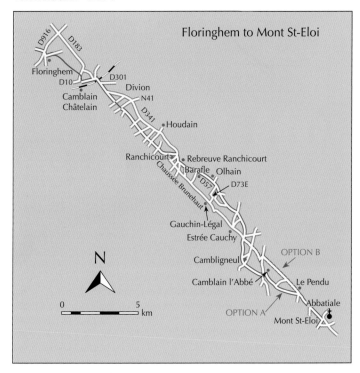

Floringhem to Mont St-Eloi

Cross over and go down D183 (**Rue Roger Salengro**), passing sitting area (R) and damaged wayside shrine. Road bends L, and after that turn R down narrow unmarked minor road at side of house 38, veering L at T-junction shortly afterwards. Continue on unsurfaced road between fields, with view of more pointed terrils (slag heaps) over to L ahead behind main road.

KSO, ignoring turnings, past large pond with a lot of bushes beside it (if track is flooded you can pass on bank to L). KSO, pass large wood (on L) and reach minor road on outskirts of

3km Camblain Châtelain (120/825)

Bakery, bars.

Turn L along this road, then KSO ahead to a junction with small wayside chapel. Turn R onto **Rue Pasteur**, KSO at 'stop' sign,▼ cross river and go uphill to T-junction with the D70 and then turn L along it.

Alternatively, you can turn L here to the Eglise Saint-Omer and mairie and then turn R to emerge further along D70 by war memorial.

KSO until you reach the D341 (boundary of Camblain and Calonne Ricquart). Turn R uphill and continue to entrance to

2km Divion (122/823)

Centre of town (2km from here, off route to L) has shops, banks, etc, but no accommodation apart from the campsite (at the side of the route described here).

Note as you enter Divion (and continuing along the D341) that each street has a plaque at the end with a quote by a different French author, proceeding in alphabetical order (Aragon, Baudelaire, and so on) – an attempt, perhaps, to brighten up a somewhat depessed area now that there is no longer any mining activity and/or to make a change from the former street names, which were simply 'Rue A, Rue B', etc. You will see, for example, that 'Rue G' has become 'Rue Théophile Gauthier' and 'Rue H' is now 'Rue Victor Hugo'.

At the entrance to the town the D341 (marked 'Arras 30, Houdain 4') veers L away from the straight-as-a-die line of the **Chaussée Brunehaut**, doing a 'loop' before rejoining it some 10km later after Rebreuve Ranchicourt. It is suggested that you continue straight ahead here, downhill on the Chaussée Brunehaut (take

Street-name sign, Divion

this for the campsite too). *However, as you will not pass any more shops until you reach Arras (or they may not be open when you pass), you may like to do a small detour first before continuing – follow the road round to L, veer R*

85

downhill after café-tabac (newsagent) onto Rue Jean Guesde, where there is a '8 à Huit' (superette) on your L, and then retrace your steps.

Sigeric's stage LXXVI (Bruwaei, 76) was in Bruay-la-Bussière, 5km to the east of here (4 hotels).

To continue, when you see the sign indicating 'Arras 30, Houdain 4' and a L turn at the entrance to Division, continue straight ahead, downhill, on the **Chaussée Brunehaut**. At junction at bottom KSO ahead uphill on tarmac FP past sports complex (and campsite) to the N41. Cross over and KSO ahead (quite literally). After houses stop, tarmac stops too, and FP becomes an earth track until the outskirts of

4km Houdain (126/819)

Continue straight ahead all the time. *If you want to go into the centre of Houdain, turn L at crossing with a roundabout.* Continue into the countryside and then take the third tarmac turning on L, a small tarmac road leading diagonally through fields in the direction of the church spire ahead. Follow this as it snakes its way between houses, continue on **Rue du Château** then turn R onto **Rue de la Fusion** to bring you out on the D341 again in

2km Rebreuve Ranchicourt (128/817)

Café (not always open), restaurant (in château).

Turn R, continue for nearly 1km, then fork L onto D57 (marked 'Olhain'). KSO past hamlet of **Barafle** to

2km Olhain (130/815)

Picnic area to L at entrance to village, auberge (X Sun pm and all Mon), Château d'Olhain, the only remaining *château féodale* in the area, surrounded by a moat (with water in it); visits 3.00–7.00pm Sun and holidays (03.21.27.94.76).

Continue through village and at end KSO(R) on D57 at junction (marked 'Gauchin Le Gal') with large wayside cross and then, 30–40m after next junction, with D73, turn R up grassy track to side of house. This widens out after a while and becomes an earth track. KSO, ignoring turns, for 2.5–3km, after which a small road joins from L and tarmac starts. When road veers sharp R, KSO(L) ahead on more minor road, which becomes an earth track, for 1km. Turn R at T-junction and reach D341, where you have two alternatives.

OPTION A

Cross over and continue (slighty staggered to R) on another earth track on other side for 1.5km to entrance to

6km Cambligneul (136/809)

Cross road, continue ahead to 'stop' sign (D72E2), turn L to crossing with D75 and continue on other side to

2km Camblain l'Abbé (138/807) Pop. 690

No facilities, but pilgrims with a credential can sleep in the Ecole Saint-Jean-Baptiste de la Salle, Rue Perroy 5, a Catholic boys' boarding school where they have 4 bunks in their infirmary; ring ahead 03.23.22.00.04. All year, but no meals during school holidays. No charge as such, but you should offer a donation.

Turn L at end to crossing with D341 and either turn R to continue or, to sleep in the **Ecole Saint-Jean-Baptiste de la Salle**, turn L slightly afterwards into **Rue Longineul** (signposted). *Silhouette of ruined abbey at Mont Saint-Eloi on skyline ahead.*

KSO on D341. Picnic area 400m later, on L, after junction with D58.

OPTION B

This option is slightly shorter. Turn L along the D341 here, continue for 1.5km then, as main road begins to veer R, turn L onto a very small tarmac road and then, almost immediately, R to continue on the original line of the **Chaussée Brunehaut**, straight as a die all the time. KSO ahead, on tarmac at first, then on an earth track, through woods. To sleep in the school mentioned above turn second R back to the main road and then turn L in the village up **Rue Longineul**.

Otherwise – KSO all the time. After 2km cross a minor road, continue on grassy track on the other side, passing behind a farmhouse, and emerge on the D341 again by the picnic area on its LH side.

Both routes Continue on D341 here for 2km more to

6km Mont Saint-Eloi (144/801) Pop. 1017

Bar in centre. Ruins of seventh-century abbey founded by Irish monks.

Turn R down alley to L of house 19 (waymarked as the GR127), then turn L along side of field 80m later. Reach road and turn R downhill to war memorial and large wayside cross at entrance to

0.5km Ecoivres (144.5/800.5)

Continue ahead (**Rue de la Source**) past bus shelter to church (seat) then KSO(L), veering R onto **Chemin des Normands**. Go under railway line then turn L immediately onto very minor road, turning L over bridge 400m later.

KSO ahead into **Bray** (a hamlet) and turn R (seat at junction) into **Rue d'Ecole**. Go over level crossing, turn L on other side and continue alongside railway line for 1.5km. Pass large paint factory on R then turn L over level crossing onto D56 at entrance to

3.5km Maroeuil (148/797) Pop. 2506, 65m

Bakery, 2 bars, superette in Rue de Neuville.

Veer R (**Rue de la Gare**) then L (marked 'Centre, Mairie') then turn R down **Rue du Vert Bocager** (church and small bar on main road ahead). Turn L, cross small river (**La Scarpe**), and then turn R along **Rue de la Marlière**, then R again onto **Rue de la Source**, taking you to the **Fontaine de Sainte-Bertille** (*a local saint, died 697, who, in a period of extreme drought, is said to have struck the ground with her stick and made this well appear*).

KSO ahead past the oratory, *a wayside shrine with steps down to reach the water, reputed for its ability to cure eye complaints*, then 100m later turn R under iron arch to bridge ahead (seats). Do **not** cross bridge, but turn L here alongside river. KSO for 700m and turn R along the **Rue de Maroeuil** in **Louez**.

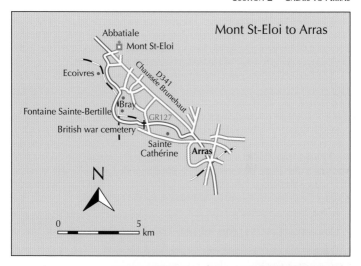

Mont St-Eloi to Arras

Fontaine Sainte-Bertille

150m later turn R at junction (auberge on opposite corner) on **Rue de la Scarpe**, crossing river again (*note restored water mill to L, complete with machinery*), veering L. 300m later turn L into **Rue des Maçons**. Go under road bridge (war cemetery uphill to R), after which the road becomes a track. KSO over open

89

land and then tree-lined path for 1.5km then, as you start to go downhill, track veers L. Follow it round (in effect, there are two paths, parallel to each other), go through turnstile gate past picnic area to **Avenue des Atrebates**, then turn R and then R again onto the D64 (which becomes the **Rue du 8 mai 1945**).

KSO for 700–800m more then turn L down **Chemin des Maçons** (not sign-posted at the start, but waymarked with red and white balises), opposite a football field. Turn R into a parking area, then L down a tree-lined avenue, turning R at the end, veering L past building with large pond in front of it. Pass to its RH side, continue ahead on other side, veering slightly L, and downhill, then turn R to pass in front of tennis courts. Veer L past building with indoor courts (do **not** cross bridge marked with the GR balises), cross another parking area and turn R into **Rue Notre-Dame de Lorette**. Reach **Rondpoint de Tchécoslovakie**, continue down **Rue Méaulens** to the cathedral, and from there continue along the **Rue des 3 Visages** and then the Rue des 3 Marteaux to the Grand'Place in

6km Arras (154/791) Pop. 40,585, 72m

Large town with all facilities, TO in hôtel de ville, Place des Héros (03.21.51.26.95, arras.tourisme@wanadoo.fr), SNCF (TGV to Paris, Lille).

Accommodation in all price brackets. YH, Grand'Place 59 (03.21.22.70.02, arras@fuaj.fr) Reasonably priced accommodation is also available in the Maison Diocésaine Saint-Vaast, Rue d'Amiens 103, 10mins walk from city centre (03.21.212.40.38, phone ahead in office hours, open all year, meals available). PS from 'Accueil' in cathedral (May–Oct only).

Good place for a day off. Arras was very heavily bombarded during the Second World War and the whole of the historic centre is, in fact, a post-war reconstruction. The main sights include the Cathedral of Saint-Vaast, the Gothic town hall and belfry, many 18th-century buildings, Citadelle Vauban and 'Les Boves', a network of underground galleries dating from the 10th century, originally chalk quarries, and covering the size of the town (guided tours only). There are also 150 British and Commonwealth war cemeteries in and around Arras.

Stage LXXV (Atherats, 75) in Sigeric's itinerary.

Looking back at Laon cathedral

ARRAS TO REIMS

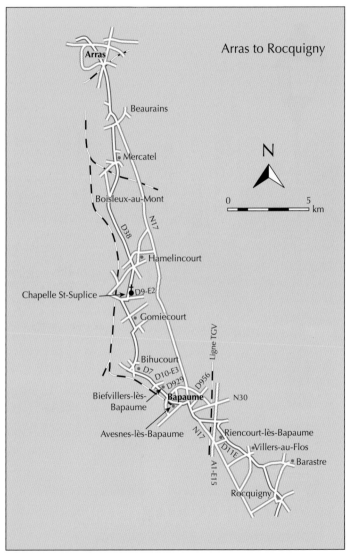

Arras to Rocquigny

A single grave...

From the **Grand'Place** (and with your back to the 3 Luppars – a hotel, and the only red-brick building in the square) cross the Grand'Place and KSO ahead along the **Rue de la Taillerie**. Continue ahead past the **Place des Héros** (*bell-tower to R has a carillon which rings every quarter of an hour, but the carilloneur himself plays every first Saturday morning in the month, 11.00–11.30am*), and then KSO along **Rue des Balances**. Turn L into **Rue Emile Legrelle** (not marked at start) which then becomes **Rue Pasteur**. Turn R at the traffic lights into **Rue Chanzy** and reach **Place Maréchal Foch** and the railway station.

Turn R in front of the station onto **Rue du Docteur Brassart**, passing SNCF buildings (L) and the **Trésor Public** (R), then turn L into the **Avenue du Maréchal Leclerc**. This becomes the **Avenue Fernand Lobbedez** and then the **Route de Bapaume**.

After leaving the boundary of the city of Arras you enter **Beaurains**, passing the **Beaumarais Road Cemetery** (*on your R – war graves, with cemetery register and visitors' book in box in wall*). 3km from Arras city centre cross the D5, after which watch out carefully for the **Rue de Robespierre**, forking off to your R just before a water tower (also on your R). Turn R here and continue straight ahead, passing under the D6.

Do not continue ahead to the roundabout, and then turn R onto the D6 there in order to try and turn L onto the minor road after that, as the embankment is difficult to climb down with a fully laden rucksack.

KSO. KSO(R) at fork and after 2km reach

4km Mercatel (158/787) Pop. 572

Seats to L by wayside chapel in centre.

KSO straight ahead (road not signposted), going under railway line and past large wayside cross by **Sunken Road Cemetery**. *(Many of the small war cemeteries out in the countryside are on the site of former military field hospitals or nearest to the place where the soldiers died.)* Continue to junction with D35 and turn R for 800m to a junction by the church in

3km Boisleux-au-Mont (161/784) Pop. 413, 88m
Café-tabac by church.

Turn L here onto D36 (**Rue de Hamelincourt**), cross **Le Cojeul** (a stream) and KSO ahead for 3km to church in

3km Hamelincourt (164/781) Pop. 254, 105m

Turn R, veering L into **Rue du Comte**, and 500m later, at crossroads by chicken farm, turn R (D12) and then fork L immediately down small unsurfaced road that then becomes a grassy track. KSO ahead for 2km until you reach a T-junction with the D9E2. Turn R along it to a staggered junction with a small wayside oratory, then turn L onto the C9, passing the brick **Chapelle Saint-Sulpice** (on R) and KSO until you reach the D9 in

Bell-tower, Bapaume

4km Gomiécourt (168/777) Pop. 174, 117m

Turn R then immediately L to **Rue de Bihucourt** and church. Continue ahead for 1km then veer R and then L on minor road. KSO(L) at junction with smaller road and KSO until you reach the entrance to

4km Bihucourt (172/773) Pop. 312

Pass to LH side of football field (seats) on **Rue de Bapaume**, passing cemetery (on L) with Commonwealth war graves, and then turn L onto the D7 for 1.5km to **Biefvillers-lès-Bapaume**. Continue ahead for 1km until you come to a big roundabout and take the turning marked 'Avesnes-lès-Bapaume' (**not** 'Bapaume Centre'), then take the first turning on the R by a very large pond. Pass mairie (of **Avesnes-lès-Bapaume**) and at 'stop' sign at end (café/resto opposite) turn L to enter

4km Bapaume (176/769) Pop. 431, 122m

SCRB. SI (TO) Place Faidherbe 31. Parish accommodation possible on floor of large hall with w/c and washbasin but no shower, Rue de l'Eglise 3 (03.21.07.13.37). (Note that it is essential to ring ahead and find out when Monsieur l'Abbé – the parish priest, who has 16 other parishes – will be there, as the secretary cannot give permission to sleep there.) *Hôtel le Gourmet, Rue de la Gare 10 (03.21.07.20.00),**Hôtel de la Paix, Avenue Abel Guidet (03.21.07.11.03), Café/tabac/hotel l'Escale on main street on way out of town.

Continue for 400m to a T-junction (large supermarket on L) then turn R marked 'Bapaume Centre', passing mairie with another *beffroi* (tall bell-tower). Continue along **Rue du Faubourg de Péronne**. 800m later turn L onto D7 (marked 'Bancourt'). Cross the railway line and then the motorway (A1-E15) and 150m later turn hard R, veering L onto minor road. KSO for 1.5km to junction in

3km Riencourt-lès-Bapaume (179/766)

KSO(L) ahead here on D11-E3, passing **Manchester Cemetery** (1914–15, 60 graves) on L, to

2km Villers-au-Flos (181/764)

German military cemetery. Here, as in all the others, there are only very austere, plain iron crosses, often with three or four names on each, in trees and/ or grass but no flowers, as there are in the Allied war cemeteries. On a clear day the countryside in the section between Bapaume and Péronne is set out in front of you like a map.

KSO at first crossroads by mairie then, at bend (church, to L, has covered seating outside) KSO(R) into **Rue de Le Transloy**. 150m later turn L on **Rue de Barastre**, passing cemetery (on R) and 'La Grotte' (on L) and KSO. 800m after, that road bends L, R and L again, but instead of continuing L to **Barastre** (church spire visible 1km ahead) when HT pylons cross telegraph wires overhead KSO(R) ahead on earth track, following line of telegraph poles. KSO for 2km to entrance to **Rocquingny**, passing cemetery on L and wayside chapel on R, to junction with D19 by large brick chapel/church in the centre of

3km Rocquingny (184/761)

Café at junction in centre (not always open).

Continue ahead, marked 'Mesnil en A' but then, before next marked junction, after house No 15, turn R down **Rue de Sailly**, veering L at junction with **Rue Bardum**. KSO, cross bridge over motorway and KSO for 2km more, heading for a very large radio transmitter on the skyline at the entrance to

4km Sailly-Saillisel (188/757) Pop. 410

Once you have crossed the motorway you have left the Pas de Calais (62) and are now in the old province of Picardie, in the *département* of the Somme (80). (It is useful to remember which one you are in, as this helps when using the telephone directory.)

Continue to crossing with D184 (children's play area to L with seats) and KSO ahead on **Rue de Péronne**. At fork KSO(L) ahead to D1017 then turn L along it for 1km to

2.5km Rancourt (190.5/754.5)

400–500m after a RH turn onto a minor road look out for a track to the L which takes you to the side of the **Bois de Saint-Pierre Vaast**, the woods that you can see to your L. 800m later turn R and pass behind the **Nécropole Nationale**, a French military cemetery, and its **Chapelle du Souvenir Français** (a very large

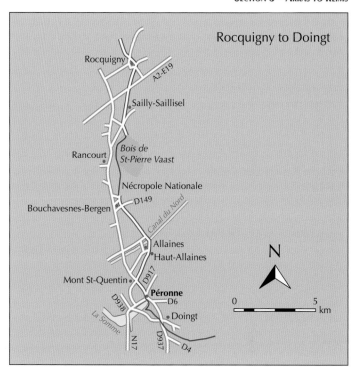

Rocquigny to Doingt

memorial church). This then brings you out on the **Rue de Bergen** at the start of **Bouchavesnes-Bergen**, where you KSO ahead to the church.

If you miss the turning, or if you find the path blocked by construction, you will have to continue on the D1017 for 2.5km more (passing Hôtel Le Prieuré, on L) and then take the first LH fork after the big cemetery, an unmarked minor road, in the general direction of the church in front of you. Turn R when you reach the junction with the Rue de Bergen and continue to the church in

2.5km Bouchavesnes-Bergen (193/752) Pop. 326

Turn L at junction by church, marked 'Moislans', but then turn R immediately up **Rue d'Allaines**. KSO for 2.5km, cross the **Canal de Nord**, veering R and then L uphill (**Rue du Pont Debray**) to the D43 and turn R along it (marked 'Péronne').

3km Allaines (196/749) Pop. 410

KSO along D43 for 2km, uphill to a large roundabout at the junction with the N17 at the **Mont Saint-Quentin** (bar, 200m to R). Do **not** turn L here (marked 'Péronne Centre' – this is for vehicles) but KSO ahead (marked 'Albert, Hôpital') on the **Rue du Mont Saint-Quentin**. Continue ahead on the **Rue Jean Toeuf**, passing the hospital, KSO on the **Avenue Charles Boulanger** and the **Rue de la Caisse d'Epargne** to the junction with the **Rue Saint-Sauveur** in the centre of

4km Péronne (200/745) Pop. 8963, 54m

Shops, banks, etc. TO Rue Louis XI 1 (03.22.84.42.38). ***Hôtel/Resto Saint-Claude, Place Louis Daudré (03.22.79.49.49),**Hôtel Campanile, Route de Paris (on outskirts, 03.22.84.22.22), Hôtel La Picardie, Rue de Faubourg de Bretagne 7 (03.22.84.02.36), Hôtel/Resto Chez Baby, Rue Béranger (near former railway station, 03.22.84.12.60). Camping du Port de Plaisance, Route de Paris (03.22.84.19.31, 1/3–31/10), Camping Municipal du Brochet. Pilgrims with a credential can contact the parish office (phone ahead, 03.22.84.16.90) for very basic accommodation (sleeping bag needed), Rue Saint-Jean 16.

Château, Péronne

Péronne was very heavily bombarded during the Second World War and most of the town has been rebuilt. Medieval château now houses the Historial de la Grande Guerre (First World War museum). Eglise Saint-Jean-Baptiste in flamboyant Gothic style. Hôtel de ville dates from 13th century, with carillon ('Madelon') chiming daily in bell-tower.

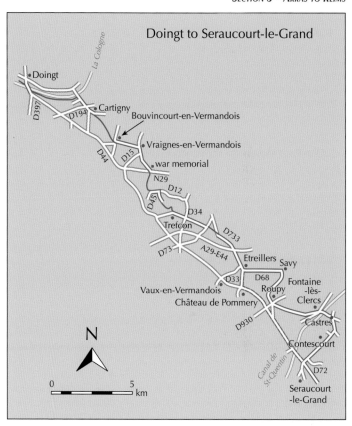

Doingt to Seraucourt-le-Grand

Cross the **Rue Saint-Sauveur** and continue ahead on the **Rue Béranger** then the **Avenue de la Gare** (D199) to former railway station, veering L and then, at bend, KSO ahead on former railway line, passing to RH side of house No 45. Cross FB over stream and KSO. Pass behind house and 200m later (and 2km from the centre of Péronne) go under road bridge. Cross minor road (café to L on outskirts of **Doingt** – *Stage LXXIV (Duin, 74) in Sigeric's itinerary*) and continue ahead behind house, on old railway line all the time. 1km later cross another minor road and KSO for 3km, until you reach the D194E on the outskirts of

4.5km Cartigny (204.5/740.5) Pop. 714

Bakery. Eglise Sainte-Radegonde.

Turn R uphill (D194), veering L at junction, then R, and continue past PO, mairie and bakery. KSO, pass wayside chapel set back from the road and turn R 100m later onto tarred, unmarked road. KSO for 2km to village of

3.5km Bouvincourt-en-Vermandois (208/737)

Turn L at junction then R to mairie, and turn R opposite on the **Rue de Vraignes** (not marked at start), passing war memorial on L. KSO for 2km to junction in

2km Vraignes-en-Vermandois (210/735)

Camping Les Hortensias, Rue Basse 22 (03.22.85.64.68), all year.

Turn R to church then fork L down **Rue Basse** (marked 'Camping'). Pass campsite (on R) and KSO to very end of street, which reaches the N29 (the **Chaussée Brunehaut** again) 1.5km later. Turn L (war memorial on L) – wide verge – then 50m later turn R up unmarked tarmac lane with fields to either side. Reach crossing of similar tracks 1km later, then 400m after that cross D45/D12 and continue ahead on cobbled lane to woods. Cross the **Omignon** (small river) and 400m later reach T-junction with a slightly bigger track. Turn L, veering R, and KSO, gently uphill all the time and ignoring turnings to L and R. Emerge from woods and continue between fields to the D345. Turn L along it for 300–400m to

4km Trefcon (214/731)

Gîte équestre Val d'Omignan, Rue Principale 3 (03.23.66.58.64), 17 places in gîte, 7 in CH, meals available. You are now in the département of the Aisne (02).

Continue through village, pass mairie (on R) and KSO ahead at junction with wayside cross. At T-junction with D73 turn L and then almost immediately R onto small unmarked road that joins another road coming from back L 800m later. KSO(R) ahead, cross motorway, then follow road round to junction by church in

5.5km Etreillers (219.5/725.5) Pop. 1106

Café-tabac opposite church, bakery, pharmacy, shop on main street.

Note *The route described here as far as Seraucourt-le-Grand is not the one suggested by the AIVF (which is meandering, on more minor roads, via Savy, Roupy, Fontaine-les-Clercs, Castres and Contescourt), but is considerably shorter (and does not normally have much traffic).*

Continue to next junction on **Rue des Docteurs** then cross the D68 and KSO for 1km. Pass under a bridge and turn L on the D32 and KSO. Pass the turning to Roupy 2km later (*note church with openwork spire over to L, typical of many in this area*), cross the D930 and KSO again. Cross the **Canal de Saint-Quentin** 4km after that, then the river **Somme**, and reach junction with **Eglise Saint-Martin**, war memorial and mairie in

6.5km Seraucourt-le-Grand (226/719)

Superette to L (does takeaway pizzas). Café. Stage LXXIII (Martinwaeth, 73) in Sigeric's itinerary.

Séraucourt-le-Grand, church and mairie

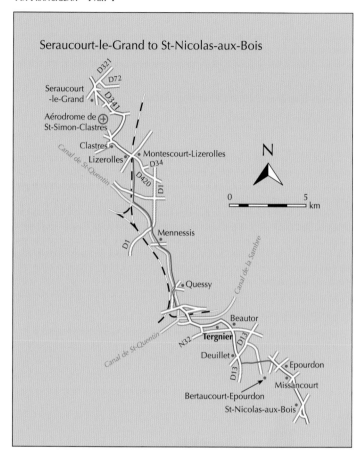

Seraucourt-le-Grand to St-Nicolas-aux-Bois

Continue ahead on **Rue Louise Lambert de la Tour** (pharmacy on R), then turn R by roadside statue onto **Rue Henry Poizot**. Turn L opposite house No 13 up road (no name at start) to L of café, veering R to crossing with the D341 and then turn L onto it, uphill in the direction of four large windmills on the skyline. Follow the road round for 5km as it skirts the airfield then, at sharp bend to R near a water tower and before you reach a road junction, KSO(L) ahead on wide grassy track which takes you to the church (with openwork spire, like the one in Roupy) in

102

5.5km Clastres (231.5/713.5) Pop. 509

Bar (to R). Seats by monument to R of church (by mairie).

Turn L on D34 and KSO ahead to

1.5km Montescourt-Lizerolles (233/712) Pop. 1476

Do **not** turn L under railway line but KSO(R) ahead on D8 (marked 'Jussy') then fork first L into **Rue Missemboeuf** (not marked at start), passing the post office. At junction fork L ito **Rue du Lt Brunehaut** and at end turn L under railway bridge. Turn R on other side on gravel track alongside railway, gently uphill all the time, and after a while it becomes a grassy track. 1km later track joins from back R (from over the bridge), and 500m after that cross a minor road. KSO on other side (marked 'sauf riverains'), veering back close to the railway line again, and 500m after that, by a railway bridge and a FB, reach the

3km Canal de Saint-Quentin (236/709)

Decide which side of the canal you would prefer to walk on (ie in the shade if it's hot) and turn L along it.

KSO! After 2km pass under a road, and 1.5km after that under the bridge at **Mennessis**, and 4.5km after that reach the bridge at

8km Quessy (244/701)

Here you leave the canal. Turn L on the other side along **Rue Anatole France** and **Rue Vaucanson**, passing SNCF station and **Rue Pierre Semard** to junction with **Boulevard G Grégoire** in

2km Tergnier (246/699) Pop. 15,289

Shops, bars, banks, pharmacy, etc. SNCF, several small hotels on road by station, including Relais des Nations, Rue Marceau 1 (03.23.57.49.79, X Sun), Hôtel des Voyageurs, Rue Semard 60 (03.28.57.20.68.) and Le Rallye, Rue Semard 52 (03.23.57.22.79). Large railway junction full of sidings, marshalling yards, etc, a sort of French version of Crewe, but no 'sights' as such.

From here the scenery starts to change a little and become hillier and wooded (Forêt de Saint-Gobain).

To go to the mairie or PO turn R under the railway line. Otherwise, to continue, turn L (**Boulevard G Grégoire**), cross the canal and then fork R into **Rue Carnot**. At roundabout with sculpture in the middle turn R into **Rue Henri Martin**, cross a canal (road becomes **Rue de la Frette**) and continue along **Rue du Mauger**.

At junction after gravel works on R turn L (C27) for 1km on **Rue Louis Lumière** to junction near a canal bridge (café-tabac to L) in

4km Beautor (250/695)

Turn R on **Grande Rue** (marked 'Deuillet, Saint-Gobain'), follow road round, crossing river, cross D1032 and continue on D533 on other side to

2.5km Deuillet (252.5/692.5)

Turn R on D13, veering L by mairie and café/tabac onto **Route de Saint-Gobain**. 300m later turn L onto small tarmac lane by village exit board (house No 17), veering L to farm, after which the lane becomes a grassy track/earth lane, gently uphill all the time and mainly shady. After 1.5km cross very minor road, continue ahead on other side, KSO(L) ahead by farm, pass football field (seats) and reach, via **Rue Jean Landrin**, a five-point junction in

2.5km Bertaucourt-Epourdon (255/690)

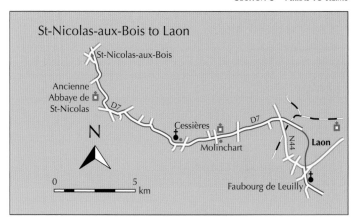

Turn second R here (**Route de Missamcourt**) and KSO ahead through **Missamcourt** (1.7km, seat by wayside cross at junction). Continue ahead here on **Route de Saint-Nicolas** (the road becomes shady after a while as you are now in the Forêt de Saint-Gobain) until you reach

6km Saint-Nicolas-aux-Bois (271/674)

12th-century church. Resto at entrance to village (X Tues, Wed).

KSO through village, KSO(R) ahead at junction (marked 'Suzy'), passing church. Pass mairie, veering L, and 1km later reach ruins of the **Benedictine Abbaye de Saint-Nicolas** (now privately owned). KSO, uphill all the time, to the

2.5km Junction with the D7 (273.5/691.5)

Turn L along it (road ahead signed 'Camping') and KSO along D7, mainly shady and mainly gently downhill to

4.5km Cessières (278/667)

Restaurant (X Sun eve, Mon, Tues), CH Rue Buet 7 (03.232.24.19.07). Seats opposite war memorial. Church of SS-Sulpice and Antoine (Gothic-Romanesque). The upper town in Laon is visible ahead on the skyline on a clear day.

KSO through village on D7 again to

3.5km Molinchart (281.5/663.5)

12th–13th-century Eglise Saint-Martin, but no facilities.

KSO on D7 for 4km, cross N44 and enter **Laon-Neuville** (the lower town) via **Rue Roger Cadeau**. At junction with **Rue de l'Enfer** turn R for campsite, otherwise KSO on **Rue Gabriel Peri**, go over level crossing, continue on **Rue Nestor Greehaut** and then fork R at **Carrefour Winchester** (*Laon is twinned with Winchester*) onto **Rue Jean-Baptiste Lebas**. Turn R up **Rampe Saint-Marcel** (a very steep street), then at house No 24 fork R up a FP which becomes **Rue de l'Eperon**. At the top turn R into **Rue Franklin Roosevelt** and at end turn L along **Rue du Bourg** to the hôtel de ville in

6.5km Laon (288/657) Pop. 28,000

All facilities, TO in Hôtel Dieu, former pilgriim hospital (in upper town, 03.23.20.28.62, info@tourisme-paysdelaon.com). SNCF (Paris, Amiens, Reims, Tergnier). Hotels include de la Paix, Rue Saint-Jean 52 (03.23.79.06.34, X Mon), La Bannière de France (both in upper town), Welcome, Avenue Carnot (03.23.23.06.11),**des Arts, Place des Droits de l'Homme 11 (03.23.79.57.16, both in lower town near station) and *Marmotte, Avenue Georges Pompidou (03.23.20.18.11). Pilgrim stamp in presbytère, Rue du Cloître 8 (side of cathedral), open Tues–Sun (X Sat pm). Launderette Place Saint-Julien 9 (in upper town).

The upper town, with the cathedral, historic centre (with almost 80 listed buildings) and a bishopric dating from the sixth century, is on a ridge 2km long and 400m wide. (The lower town grew up in the 19th century, with the arrival of the railway.) Historically the town is well known for the 'Sept

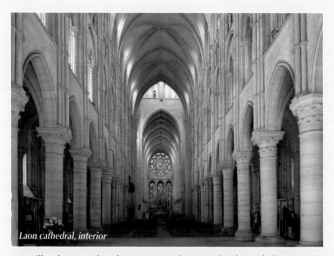

Laon cathedral, interior

Merveilles de Laon', listed in a pre-Revolutionary book entitled *Le Laonnais Pittoresque*, and these comprise the cathedral; the abbey churches of Saint-Martin and Saint-Vincent; the pond belonging to the monks of Saint-Vincent, whose water level never goes down; the Tour Penchée de Dame Eve; the Os qui Pend (half a whale's jawbone brought from England in 1113 and hung in the cathedral porch in the 13th century); and the Pierre à Clous, a stone with three nails in it, dating from 1338.

Early Gothic cathedral (note the colossal stone ox at the top of its towers – legend has it that during the construction of the cathedral a yoke of oxen was having difficulty hauling its heavy load of stone up the hill when a mysterious ox appeared to help and then disappeared as soon as they reached the top). The town's other mains sights include the Eglise Saint-Martin-au-Parvis, the Hôtel Dieu (12th-century hospital), Palais Episcopal and the Eglise Abbatiale Saint-Martin. Good place for a rest day (guided walking tour recommended – ask in TO). Stage LXXII (Mundlothuin, 72) in Sigeric's itinerary.

The POMA is a funicular from the railway station (in the lower town) to the hôtel de ville (in the upper town), Mon–Sat only. Closed part of July/Aug for annual maintenance, but then replaced by a bus service. Otherwise you can go up the Escalier Municipal, from the lower town (near the station) to the upper, but it has 295 steps!

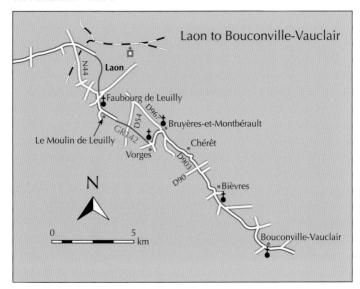

Laon to Bouconville-Vauclair

Laon
Faubourg de Leuilly
Bruyères-et-Montbérault
Le Moulin de Leuilly
Chérêt
Vorges
Bièvres
Bouconville-Vauclair

N

0   5 km

Backtrack from the hôtel de ville and go back along the **Rue du Bourg**. Continue along the **Rue Saint-Jean**, pass **Place Saint-Julien** and continue along the **Rue Saint-Martin** to the church (**Eglise Abbatiale Saint-Martin**). Continue ahead along the **Rue de la Libération** to the **Porte de Soissons**, and then take the second RH turn (at the IUT – part of the Université de Picardie) down the **Ruelle de la Vieille Montagne**, a grassy track waymarked as the GR142 (which you follow all the way to Vorges, so watch out for balises), which leads steeply downhill to the junction by the church and former tollhouse in

1km Semilly (289/656)

Turn L here along **Rue Romanette** (marked 'Cimitière allemande') past small church then, 300m later, by house No 20, turn R on very minor road leading to the N2 400m later. Cross over, KSO on other side, veering R. KSO(R) by wayside cross on bigger road coming from back L, then turn L on **Rue de Coq** to church and square in

2km Leuilly (291/654)

Eglises de Notre-Dame et Saint-Eloi, 16th century.

Veer L in front of church then R along **Rue de la Ferme**. 300m later cross small river (**L'Ardon**), then 100m after that, by sharp RH bend, turn L by barn, veering R towards woods ahead. Enter woods and then turn **third** L on the other side of the ditch. *(This section can be very muddy, even in summer, but improves as you go along.)* 700m later wide grassy track joins from back R. KSO(L) ahead along it for 300m to minor road and turn L.

100m later turn R down wide grassy lane to L of big house. KSO for 1.5km, continuing at end on **Chemin de la Christopherre**, which then becomes **Avenue de Vincennes** and a junction in

4km Vorges (295/650) Pop. 387

Boulangerie.

Turn L (*to visit large Gothic Eglise Saint-Jean Baptiste continue ahead then retrace your steps*) and KSO on **Rue du Docteur Ganault** (the D25, Bruyères–Montbérault). Leave Vorges, gradually veering R, the road becoming **Rue Arsène Houssaye** (*note a fountain by house No 20*), and KSO to junction with D967 in the centre of

1km Bruyères-et-Montbérault (292/653) Pop. 1500

8 à Huit (shop), café, bakery, pharmacy. 12th–15th-century Eglise Notre-Dame (has 13th-century frescoes).

Turn R past church and mairie and continue along the main street, the **Rue Porte de Laon**, which becomes **Rue Porte de Reims** (D967 in the direction of 'Monthenault'), for 400m, then turn L onto the D903 (the RH of two forks) marked 'Chérêt' and 'Chambres d'Hôte'.

200m later, at bend, you have a choice – continue on the D903 or fork L, parallel to road, onto a quieter road, signed in green and yellow as a local FP, mainly shady and easy to follow, that returns to the D903 as you enter

2km Chérêt (294/651)

CH and resto, Rue Principale 18 (03.23.24.80.64).

Pass CH on L, church (porch for shelter in bad weather, fountain and seat on L) and sign for restaurant (La Petite Campagne, 03.223.24.78.63) and turn R by mairie (marked 'Bièvres'), uphill. At top reach junction with D90 *(if you turn round here you can see Laon cathedral on the skyline on a clear day)* and KSO ahead on D890 (marked 'Bièvres'), undulating for 2km to

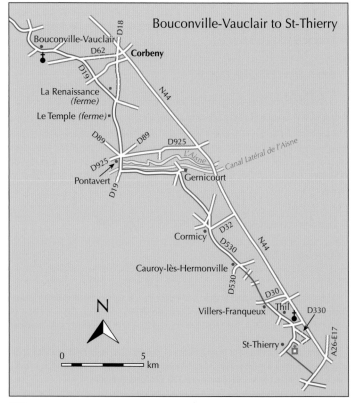

5km Bièvres (299/646)

KSO at crossing by mairie, a staggered junction on D88 (marked 'Ployart'), then 700m later cross the **Bièvre** (a small river). 100m after that KSO(R) at fork on 'C' road (marked 'Chermizy Ailles'), uphill. Pass turn on R to **Ferme de Vercaigne** and KSO uphill.

When you get almost to the top, by a 'mini-quarry' to R, watch out carefully for the red and white balises of the GR12, which crosses the road (staggered) here. It comes from the R slightly further along and continues, to your L, on a clear track along the side of a field (to L) and woods (to R) then with fields to both sides. *Splendid views on a clear day.* KSO ahead for 1km to a wayside cross, where another track joins from back L. KSO(R) ahead, veering R towards woods. Follow track round, and 2km later reach minor road at **La Bove** (château). Turn R here and continue for nearly 2km to

6km Bouconville-Vauclair (305/640)

Seats by mairie. Bar/resto L'Auberge de Vauclair.

Continue through village on D19 and KSO. 2.5km later fork L onto the D62. *(However, if you are cycling and/or do not want to sleep in Corbeny, you can KSO on the D19 here as far as Pontavert.)* Otherwise, KSO on D622, gradually uphill. Reach junction with D18 and continue for 400m to mairie, church and N44 in

5.5km Corbeny (310.5/634.5)

PO, shop, bakery, pharmacy, **Hôtel du Chemin des Dames, with bar/tabac, offers a substantial pilgrim discount on production of your credential (mention this when phoning ahead: 03.23.23.95.70). They also own the Grill Picard, a restaurant, on the main road (Rue de Laon 22). Stage LXXI (Corburnei, 71) in Sigeric's itinerary.

Backtrack 250m to junction with D18 and turn L (marked 'Pontavert'). Pass first junction then, at second (where the **Chemin des Dames** turns R), KSO ahead on D889. *(The Chemin des Dames was a key battlefield throughout World War I, particularly known for the Second Battle of the Aisne in April 1917 at which*

111

Canal near Cormicy

the French lost over 270,000 men.) At next junction this becomes the D19. KSO, ignoring turnings (6km in all, not a lot of traffic). 300m before village pass wayside shrine with seat and three large, shady trees and continue ahead into centre of

6.5km Pontavert (317/628)
Bakery.

Cross **D925** and KSO on other side (D19, marked 'Roupy'). Pass church and bakery, then 400m later cross the river **L'Aisne**. 200m after that reach the **Canal Latéral de l'Aisne**. Cross over, then turn L on the towpath on other (south) side. Continue to first bridge – but after this the towpath was completely impassable at the time this guide was being prepared.

However, instead of continuing for 2.5km more and then turning L into **Gernicourt** (see below) you can turn R and then L to continue alongside the LH side of a field (the canal is now below you to your L). This joins a proper track that then veers R and leads into the centre of

3km Gernicourt (320/625)

Turn R at mairie (seat) towards church, but then turn L up grassy track by wayside cross (**Rue du Calvaire**) and emerge on road at top, past church. Turn hard L immediately onto wide, clear earth track that leads (literally) in a straight line to Cormicy (visible ahead).

3km Cormicy (323/622)

Tabac/presse, pharmacy, bakery but no café. You are now in the département of the Marne (51).

Reach D380 on outskirts of village and turn R to junction. KSO here to another junction (turn L to church and public garden with shady seats) and KSO past pharmacy on D530. KSO for 3km to

3km Cauroy-lès-Hermonville (326/619)

When road bends sharp L at entrance to village KSO on unsurfaced road (**Rue Jeanne d'Arc**, but not marked at start), cross the D530 then continue ahead on **Rue Paul Despiques** (picnic tables to R), and when houses stop KSO ahead on wide grassy track *(tip of church spire and mairie in Villers-Franqueux visible on the skyline ahead)*, veering L and then R when another track joins from back L. KSO ahead and when track bends sharp L KSO ahead in front, over small stream (**Beaucourt**), and then up shady tarred lane ahead. 400m later cross very minor tarred road and KSO ahead, gently uphill, to five-point junction by war memorial and mairie in

3km Villers-Franqueux (329/616)

You are now in the Champagne country, with *caves/celliers* everywhere. Shady area with seats by mairie.

KSO ahead at junction on **Rue de Thil** (D330) to

2.5km Thil (331.5/613.5)

Enter village, pass church (L) and mairie, continue to end of village then turn R into **Rue de Saint-Thierry**, uphill. KSO and reach T-junction in

1.5km Saint-Thierry (333/612) Pop. 570, 145m

Bar/resto, pharmacy, Monastère des Bénédictines has accommodation but phone ahead (03.26.03.10.41). CH Harlaut-Paris, Rue Paradis 5 (03.26.03.10.72).

Note It is still another 10km to the centre of Reims (with no shops or cafés en route), so you may like to consider, if you are tired or it is getting late, staying here and then walking the remaining 2–2½hrs into Reims the following morning.

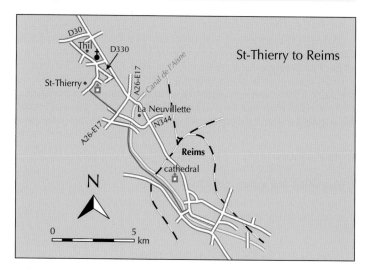

Having reached the T-junction (via **Rue Moulin**) turn R (marked 'Merfy') past the pharmacy, bar/resto and the monastery and continue through the village *(view of Reims ahead to L)*, passing the CH at 5 **Rue Paradis**. Reach a 'stop' sign (football field diagonally opposite) and turn L downhill on **Allée des Gaillerandes**. KSO ahead for 3km between fields to motorway (tarmac becomes earth track), turning R alongside it and then veering L to go up and cross bridge over it. KSO ahead on other side.

900m later, at junction, turn R (marked 'Déchetterie' – rubbish tip). 400m after that reach another junction (where you would turn R if you wanted to go to the *déchetterie*). Go towards the bridge over the canal, but then pass to its RH side, turn R and continue on the towpath to the RH side of the **Canal Latéral de l'Aisne** for 2.5km.

Pass the first railway bridge then, at the second, shortly afterwards, cross over to the other side of the canal via a pedestrian footbridge if you want to go into the city centre and/or sleep in the YH, as after that the towpath continues hemmed in by the canal on the L and a fast main road on the R, with no means of leaving it for the next three bridges.

Having crossed the canal continue on the LH bank, past **Centre des Congrés** (on L), a very large conference centre, and then go up some steps onto the **Pont de Vesle**. Turn L to go up the **Rue de Vesle** in the direction of the cathedral (which you can see ahead of you), turning seventh R along **Rue du Trésor**, for the cathedral, or R to cross the bridge to the YH (which is on the other side of the river, next to the **Comédie de Reims**, a theatre).

10km Reims (343/602) Pop. 187,201, 83m

Large town with all facilities. SNCF (trains to Paris, Nancy). Accommodation in all price brackets, including Centre International de Séjour (CIS, YH) across the river by the theatre (03.26.40.52.60, info@cis-reims.com). In the centre of Reims pilgrims can also stay in the Maison Diocésaine Saint-Sixte, Rue du Lieutenant Herduin 6 (03.26.82.72.50) and, on the outskirts, in the Monastère Saint-Claire, Rue Beregovoy 2, Cormenteuil (03.26.86.95.12). No campsite in Reims itself – the nearest one (eg for cyclists) is to the southeast, 6km off route to the east from Verzy (see below), Rue Routoir 8, 03.26.03.91.79. TO next to cathedral (03.26.77.45.00, info@reims-tour-isme.com). PS available in Maison Notre-Dame, the office at RH side of cathedral, also information on pilgrim-only accommodation.

Cathédrale de Notre-Dame, with exceptional stained-glass windows dating from the 13th century to the present day and including 2300 sculptures, open all day every day; masses 8.00am weekdays and Mon, Wed, Fri at 7.00pm. Guided visit of cathedral towers available. Reims's other main sights include the Palace des Tau, formerly the residence of the archbishops of Reims, now housing the cathedral museum, and the Romanesque-Gothic Basilique Saint-Remi, where the baptism of Clovis and 3000 warriors took place (open 8.00am–7.00pm in summer, 8.00am–5.00pm in winter; masses 8.45am and 11.15am (Sun), 8.30am (Mon and Wed), 7.00pm (Thurs). Eglise

Reims cathedral, east end

Saint-Jacques has statues of Saint James on west front and also in Passage Saint-Jacques by church, and modern abstract stained-glass windows by the Czech painter Sima. Other churches include Saint-Maurice (open Tues 10.00am–12.00pm; masses Sun 10.00am and Sat 6.00pm (6.30pm in summer), Tues and Fri 9.00am) and Saint-Laurent (open Wed afternoon, Sun mass 10.00am). Stage LXX (Rems, 70) in Sigeric's itinerary.

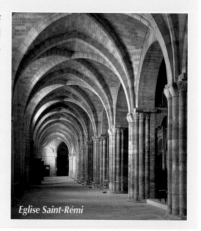

Eglise Saint-Rémi

REIMS TO BESANÇON

Vineyards near Verzenay

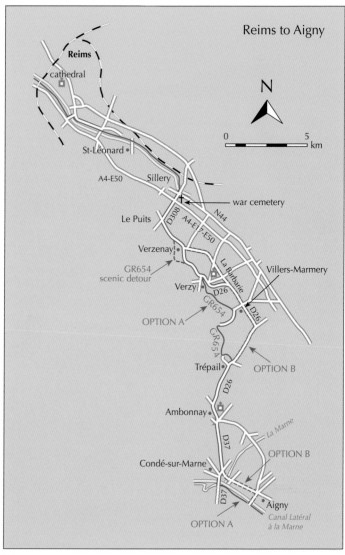

Reims to Aigny

N

0   5 km

Reims

cathedral

St-Léonard

A4-E50   Sillery

war cemetery

Le Puits

D308   A4-E17-E50   N44

Verzenay

GR654
scenic detour

La Barbarie

Villers-Marmery

Verzy

D26

GR654

OPTION A

D26

GR654

OPTION B

Trépail

D26

OPTION B

Ambonnay

La Marne

D37

OPTION B

Condé-sur-Marne

D37

Aigny

OPTION A

Canal Latéral
à la Marne

SECTION 4

Reims to Besançon (341km)

To leave Reims and continue, from the cathedral walk down the **Rue Hincmar** to the canal, turn L along **Boulevard Doumer** to the **Pont de Venise** (the fourth bridge after the second railway bridge), turn R over it and then immediately L down some concrete steps on the south (LH) side of the bridge onto the towpath. *By the second bridge after that, by the lock, you will find the balises (red and white way-marks of the Chemin de Saint-Jacques de Compostelle) and a notice telling you that it is now 2400km to Santiago. From here until shortly after Brienne-la-Vieille the two routes share many paths in common.*

The canal through Reims and as far as Saint-Léonard has plenty of seats! KSO on the towpath to

6.5km Saint-Léonard (349.5/595.5) Pop. 77, 82m

Bar/resto/hotel on R immediately after bridge.

Continue on towpath until you reach the marina in

3.5km Sillery (353/592) Pop. 165

Cyclists can stay on the towpath most of the way to Châlons-en-Champagne if they want to.

Canal towpath after Reims

Pass the lock, sports field on R, and go under the road bridge. When you reach the marina office and the *bloc sanitaire* (VF sign here) turn R into **Rue Jacques Cartier**, then L and then R into the **Rue du Mailly** (the D308). Verzernay is visible ahead L on hillside.

Cross motorway then the railway line, and then turn L at crossroads at **Le Puits** (*cru*/vineyard to visit) onto a more minor road through vines. *Moulin de Verzernay on hill to R ahead on hillside. The woods ahead R are the Fôret de la Montagne de Reims.*

About 1km before Verzernay the GR turns R off the road to do a 'scenic detour' and visit the **Moulin de Verzernay** (visible ahead R). Unless you particularly want to see this (good views), KSO ahead on road here then at fork take RH option,▼ which will lead you to the fontaine in the centre of Verzenay.

However, if you do not want to visit either Verzenay or Verzy (cyclists, for example) you can KSO here *(this section of road is called La Barbarie)* and continue (much less hilly) on the D26 to Villiers-Marmery.

You are now in 'Champagne land', square mile after square mile of neat rows of vines on south-facing slopes, with sophisticated machinery for pruning them. The names of the vineyards/celliers of the different crus (vintage wines) are usually displayed at the edge of the fields, and although at the entrance to most villages there is a list of producers/sellers where you can buy them, there are rarely any cafés!

Verzenay

5.5km Verzernay (358.5/586.5) Pop. 1100

Bar, bakery, pharmacy. CH Rue des Grossats 9 (03.26.49.43.21). PO. Musée de la Vigne (X Mon).

KSO ahead on the road to

2km Verzy (360.5/584.5) Pop. 1068, 24m

Bar, resto, bank, bakery, PO, etc. CH at junction (Pierre/Véronique Barbier Earl, du Thilhia), Rue du Louvois 1, at entrance to village on R (03.26.97.90.29 or 03.26.97.60.00, athoso997@aol.com). CH Rue Carnot 19 (M. Lallement, 03.26.97.92.32). Parish accommodation Maison pastorale, Rue Carnot (03.26.49.43.21, contact M. Alain Michel or Mme Deville).

At the 'stop' sign at the entrance to the village you have two options.

OPTION A

If you want to continue to Trépail by the most direct route (ie missing out Villers-Marmery) turn R here and then turn second L on the **Rue de la Croix de Mission** (D34). 1km later fork L at the junction by the **Chapelle de Saint-Basle**. This road then runs into the GR141/654, leading to Trépail (see below).

OPTION B

If you want to visit Verzy KSO downhill on **Rue Ernest Graingault** (D26). Pass **Eglise Saint-Basle** then veer R then L to square by mairie and shops, etc. From there KSO along **Rue Chanzy** and KSO on D26 to

3km Villers-Marmery (363.5/581.5)

Hôtel Soleil d'Or (03.26.97.95.80) + bar/resto (meals midday only), boulangerie/épicerie (7.00am–1.00pm, X Wed), tabac/presse.

KSO on road (D26, seats at end of village) for 4km to

3.5km Trépail (367/578)

Notice board at start of village announces bakery and épicerie (PS).

Both routes Continue ahead for 3km (on D26) to

3km Ambonnay (370/575)

CH (M/Mme Meuret, 03.26.57.01.13), tabac/presse, superette. Note that there are no more shops now until you reach Châlons-en-Champagne, 20km later.

Church originally dedicated to Saint-Rémi, but changed to Saint-Réol (the 26th Archbishop of Reims), built originally in the 12th century by the Moines Templiers de la Commanderie de Jérusalem. Romanesque-Gothic, with 16th-century baptismal font. Fountain in centre of Ambonnay was installed in 1865, unique of its kind, in Napoleon III style.

Sitting area at entrance to village. Here, as in many other villages along the way, you will see notice boards announcing that this is a 'Village fleuri'. The village is classified according to how well kept/planted with flowers and the like it is, based on the results of an annual competition, something along the lines of the 'best-kept village' awards in Britain.

KSO ahead on road through village, passing main square with fountain (see above). Turn L into **Rue Saint-Vincent** (auberge on corner) and KSO, passing superette and then church *(you can see inside through the grille)*. Turn R at end of **Rue Saint-Vincent** onto the D37 (signposted 'Condé-sur-Marne') and KSO for 4km to junction at edge of

4km Condé-sur-Marne (374/571)

CH, Rue Albert Barre 7 (03.26.67.95.49), *Hôtel Soleil d'Or (03.26.67.98.97), bakery, café, PO. Splendid market hall (with covered seats) in centre of square.

KSO at junction and reach roundabout shortly afterwards. Here you have two options.

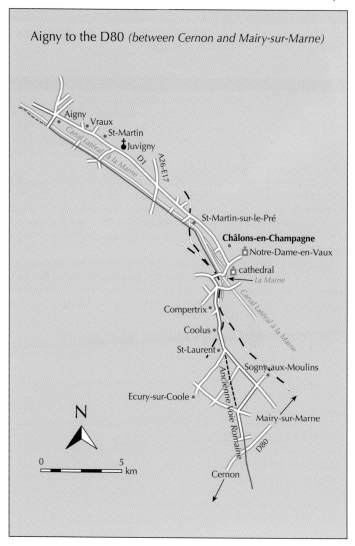

Aigny to the D80 *(between Cernon and Mairy-sur-Marne)*

OPTION A

KSO here, direction 'Jâlons' (on D37), for 400–500m to cross the **Canal Latéral à la Marne** and then turn L to KSO on its towpath.

OPTION B

Turn L here into village, pass hotel, cross another canal by lock, but as you can't access the towpath on the other side of the **Canal Latéral à la Marne** because of the T-junction of the two canals you will have to continue on the D1 (track to its LH side) for 2km for **Aigny** and then turn R down Rue de l'Eglise. Veer L, pass church, then continue ahead over bridge over (probably dried-up) river, then 200m later go over canal bridge. Turn L and KSO along the towpath.

Both routes Pass the bridge and lock in **Vraux** (2km), another bridge 1km later and then another one. Pass the lock at **Juvigny** (4km) and 2km later go under the motorway bridge. Go under two more road bridges then a railway bridge, after which you reach the road bridge at **Saint-Martin-sur-le-Pré** (7km). *From here the canal banks begin to get built up, and Châlons cathedral is visible ahead on the skyline.*

Continue for 2km more, pass under a FB then, 400m after that, turn R up steps onto bridge by roundabout between **Rue de la Marne** (L) and **Rue Jean-Jaurès** (R). *(Bicycles – go under bridge here then go up slope to RH side of lock.)* Turn L at top (useful street plan at end of bridge) to visit town centre in

---

20km Châlons-en-Champagne (394/551) Pop. 47,339, 83m

All facilities, SNCF. Accommodation in all price brackets, YH L'Embellie, 6 Rue Kellerman (near prison), all year, s/c K, 6.00pm–9.00pm (03.26.68.13.56, aj.chalons@gnu-rox.org). Camping Municipal, Rue de Plaisance (03.26.68.38.00). TO, just off Rue du Marne (03.26.65.17.89, off.tourisme.chalons-en-champagne@wanadoo.fr), has useful *visite éclair* ('lightning visit') leaflet for a 2–3hr walking tour of town.

Town dating from Gallo-Roman times, situated on the Via Agrippa (Milan-Boulgne-sur-Mer). In 1998 it reverted back – from Châlons-sur-Marne – to its original (pre-Revolutionary) name. PS in Notre-Dame-en-Vaux (staff on duty daily, am and pm). The main sights include the Cathédrale Saint-Etienne (12th–17th centuries); the Romanesque (former collegiate) church of Notre-Dame-en-Vaux (PS, Accueil daily, am and pm) with 16th-century glass and the largest set of church bells (56) in Europe; Eglise Saint-Alpin (12th–16th centuries); Eglise Saint-Jean (11th–17th centuries); and the Eglise

Square in Châlons-en-Champagne
with half-timbered houses

Saint-Loup (14th–15th centuries). Six museums. Several half-timbered houses in the town centre, typical of those you will see from here onwards. Stage LXIX (Chateluns, 69) in Sigeric's itinerary.

To continue, retrace your steps to the roundabout and cross bridge over the **Marne** and the railway line. Continue on **Rue Jean-Jaurès** then turn L onto **Rue du Lieutenant Poyer** at roundabout. At junction with lights turn second L into **Rue Basse de Compertrix** (marked 'Autres Directions' and 'Compertrix'), then at next junction, 600m, by sawmill, KSO(L) ahead (signed 'Compertrix, Coolus') on D2, alongside railway line to junction in

2km Compertrix (396/549)

At junction D2 turn R. KSO(L) ahead here past church, on **Rue du Village** (D87, CH at 8). At end of village veer R then L, marked 'Coolus, Chapelle Saint Gibrien'. Pass **Chapelle Saint-Gibrien** on L (seat). *Saint-Gibrien de Coolus was an*

Irish saint, died AD509, and his remains are now in the Eglise Saint-Rémi in Reims.
Cross railway line and enter

2km Coolus (398/547)

At junction turn R past mairie (sitting area on L). 300m later turn L at junction (onto the D2), then 1km later reach junction (Saint-Laurent) with the D4, where the **Ancienne Voie Romaine** leaves to its L shortly afterwards, straight as a die, until it joins the D4 from the back in Vésingneul-sur-Coole 17km later. However, as the first part has been ploughed up you will need to fork L here onto the D2 for 3km, to the turning to **Sogny-aux-Moulins** (signposted and 1.5km over to your L). Turn R here on a wide clear track between fields, towards woods and modern windmills ahead. After 2km reach minor tarmac road, passing in front of woods and a small isolated building perched on top of a hillock to R. Turn R onto tarmac road, but then turn L immediately onto the **Voie Romaine** (to RH side of woods), leading straight ahead, up and down, towards a group of modern windmills on the horizon. KSO!

Note *The wind can be very strong in this section and will probably be in your face all the time.*

Cross a very minor road 2km later, the D80 1km after that, and 4km later, by wind farm, cross the D54. 2km after that the D79 crosses diagonally. Here you can either **a)** fork R here and continue for 1.5km to **Fontaine-sur-Coole** *(Stage LXVIII (Funtaine, 68) in Sigeric's itinerary)* and then turn L and continue for 1.5km more on the D4 or **b)** KSO ahead, cross a minor road 800m later and then KSO again for 2km more to

17km Vésigneul-sur-Coole (415/530)

Here the Roman road runs into the D4 at the junction by the telephone box.
KSO ahead R at fork, on D4. Otherwise KSO ahead to the crossing with the N4 in

7km Coole (422/523)

Bar/resto on main road (not always open Sundays).

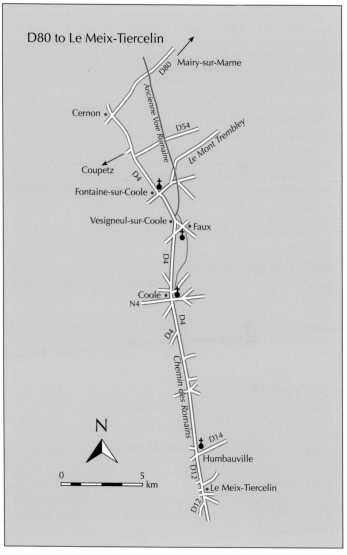

D80 to Le Meix-Tiercelin

Mairy-sur-Marne

D80

Ancienne Voie Romaine

Cernon

D54

Le Mont Trembley

Coupetz

D4

Fontaine-sur-Coole

Vesigneul-sur-Coole

Faux

D4

Coole

N4

D4

D4

Chemin des Romains

N

0   5 km

D14

Humbauville

D12

Le Meix-Tiercelin

D12

Cross N43 and continue ahead on D4 (signposted 'Sompuis') on **Rue de Sompuis**. After 1.5km D4 veers R, but KSO(L) ahead here towards the woods (**Forêt de Vauhalaise**). Cross very minor road, but then watch out as 200m later the track does a sharp bend to the R. Turn R here but then do **not** turn L onto a big track coming from the R, but cross this and then turn L on other side, downhill, behind hedge. Turn R 100m later to pick up the Voie Romaine again. KSO until you reach

10km Humbauville (432/513)

Here the tarmac starts again. Eglise Notre-Dame, part 14th century, with Romanesque tower.

Across the road from the church, house 18 Grande Rue has a scallop shell on the gatepost; if you run out of water, for example, its owners have indicated that they will be pleased to fill up your water bottle for you if they are at home.

KSO ahead (you are now on the D12) until you reach

2km Le Meix-Tiercelin (434/511)

No facilities except CH: Mme Collombar, Grande Rue 7 (03.26.72.40.37).

KSO on road through village then, 500m later, when D12 bends R, KSO(L) ahead on the **Voie Romaine** (very stony, loose gravel, and difficult to pick up much speed). KSO ahead (quite literally) to

7km Corbeil (441/504)

Café-tabac on main road to L in village. Seats by mairie.

Cross D55 and KSO ahead (**Rue Haute des Romains**) then KSO for 9km to

9km Donnement (450/495)

12th–16th-century Eglise Saint-Amand, with 16th-century stained glass. You are now in the département of the Aube (10). Stage LXVII (Domaniant, 67) in Sigeric's itinerary.

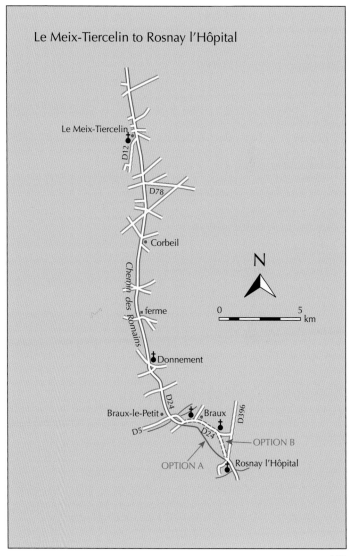

Le Meix-Tiercelin to Rosnay l'Hôpital

Le Meix-Tiercelin

D12

D78

Corbeil

Chemin des Romains

ferme

N

0   5 km

Donnement

D24

Braux-le-Petit

Braux

D396

D5

D24

OPTION B

OPTION A   Rosnay l'Hôpital

At the entrance to the village the D24 joins from back R. Turn L (**Rue de Dampierre**) then KSO at crossroads on **Rue de Braux** (D24) to

3km Braux-le-Petit (453/492)

Turn R then immediately L on **Rue du Moulin** over **Le Grand Ravel** (a small river). At the next junction you can either

(**Option A**) continue ahead on earth track, directly to **Rosnay**, ignoring any turns to L or R, joining the D24 (on your L) just before the entrance to the village or, in bad weather,

(**Option B**) follow road round to the centre of **Braux** (1.5km) then, at junction, fork R for 1.5km to **Yèvres-le-Petit** and KSO through village for 2km more to

5km Rosnay l'Hôpital (458/487)

Café-tabac (open every day X Tues). Ask in mairie about simple place to sleep. Commanderie de l'Ordre de l'Hôpital, 1650. 12th-century Eglise Notre-Dame consecrated by Saint Thomas-à-Becket.

Turn R at junction onto D398 then turn L immediately onto **Rue Saint-Jacques** (marked 'Putterville 3') which then becomes the **Rue du Long**. Cross river (**La Voire**, noting lavoir to R, useful shelter in bad weather). When the D24 does a sharp bend to L KSO(R) ahead on **Rue des Carrières**, past a sand extraction plant. Turn R at the end onto the D180, and when this veers R KSO(L) on unsurfaced road for 100m to the D398. Turn L and KSO for 6km to the entrance to the town (*the château appears on the skyline as you approach*).

After the town place-name boards turn R up **Avenue Pasteur**. Turn second L into **Rue de l'Ecole Militaire**, passing church (on L) and arriving in **Place de l'Hôtel de Ville** in

9km Brienne-le-Château (457/488) Pop. 3336, 126m

SCRB. TO Rue de l'Ecole Militaire 34 (03.25.92.82.41, open 7 days/week until 6.30pm, officetourisme.brienne@wanadoo.fr); ask here PS and also for *gîte-pèlerin*, where they have the key to a small municipally run pilgrim shelter on the way out of town in the direction of Bar-sur-Aube with

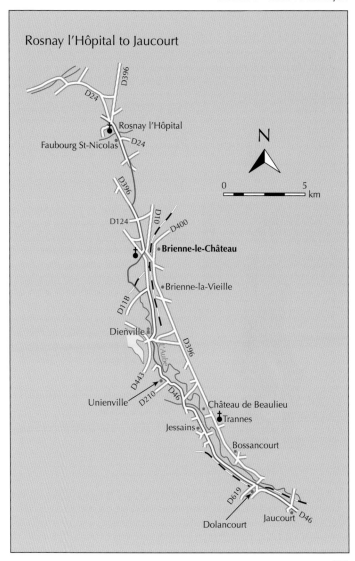

Rosnay l'Hôpital to Jaucourt

4 beds, shower, hotplate, crockery/cutlery and pans, sink; key on presentation of pilgrim passport/credential; no charge, no reservations possible, strictly on a 'first come, first served' basis. Hôtel des Voyageurs, Avenue Pasteur 30 (03.25.92.83.61) and Hôtel Croix Blanche, 7 Avenue Pasteur (03.25.92.08.27). Campsite.

Eglise des Saints Pierre et Paul, built AD1000 onwards, with 4 11th-century columns, 14th-century nave and façade). Ancienne Ecole Militaire (now the Musée Napoléon), founded 1776 and where Napoléon himself studied from 1779 to 1784, château, spendid market hall (probably 17th–18th centuries) in Place de la Halle.

Napoleon statue, Brienne-le-Château

KSO along **Rue de l'Ecole Militaire**, pass TO (on R) and then turn R up **Rue Jules Ferry**, veering L and then R to junction at end with **Rue Julien Regnier**. Turn L.

Go over level crossing then turn R immediately through red and white barrier onto grassy track through fields (marked in yellow and white as a PR (petite randonnée) route), veering away from railway line. At end KSO along street (**Allée du Pont aux Bois**) then turn R at 'stop' sign onto the D11B (**Rue du Vieux Moulin**) on the outskirts of

3km Brienne-la-Vieille (460/485) Pop. 420, 126m

12th–16th-century Eglise Saint-Pierre. Stage LXVI (Breone, 66) in Sigeric's itinerary.

Cross bridge over the river **L'Aube** and 800m later, at the top of the hill, turn L onto a grassy track in woods, waymarked with both GR and PR signs. 150m later watch out for a turning on the RH side through trees, and 150m after that cross ditch and turn L onto clear grassy track that veers L then R. Pass under HT cables, and at end of woods veer L alongside field (on your R) with woods to L.

Track improves as you proceed. Follow it round and at end veer L downhill onto a road that becomes the **Ruelle des Crapauds**. Turn R at end onto **Rue du Val** and continue to junction by bridge over the **L'Aube** in

3km Dienville (463/482)

Camping Le Tertre, Route de Radonvilliers (by bridge) (03.25.92.26.50); also has CH. Café/tabac, bar/resto, PO, bakery.

For church (those in this area are normally open), café, etc, turn L over bridge then retrace your steps to continue.

However, you can, instead, if you wish, pick up the GR654 as it crosses the bridge at the entrance to the town and which wends it way along the side of the Aube all the way to Unienville, but this is both longer and likely to be very wet and muddy.

Turn R by bridge (or L if you have visited the town), then immediately L on the D46 marked 'Unienville' on **Rue de la Pellière**, and KSO to junction by church in

3km Unienville (466/479)

Gîte d'étape (may be groups only) on main street by first fountain. 2 public fountains. Eglise Saint-Symphorien, 12th century, with large wooden porch.

Continue on road, which veers L by church (**Rue Saint-Vézard**), then R at junction, then L through hamlet of **L'Autremonde** (although you are only in this 'Other World' for 100m…). KSO on D46, often shady and mainly quiet. Cross canal and continue to

4.5km Jessains (470.5/474.5)

Bar/resto in centre (but not always open?). Camping municipal, Rue Saint-Nicolas 2. 12th-century Eglise de Saint-Pierre-ès-Liens.

KSO ahead again on D46, much of it alongside the railway line above to R. 500m before Dolancourt the N19 crosses the railway line, in front of you. Veer L and then R along the verge of the N19 for 200m, then turn L and then R onto **Rue de la Vallée de Landion** (seats) to shady square in the centre of

5km Dolancourt (475.5/469.5)

Eglise Saint-Léger, 12th century in part but altered in the 14th.

Turn L behind church on **Rue du Vannaye** (D44), cross river and veer R past lavoir. KSO to

2.5km Jaucourt (478/467)

KSO through village and KSO again. (Fountain opposite road KM 16.) Continue to

5km Proverville (483/462)

Eglise Saint-Genêt, 12th and 15th centuries.

Eglise Saint-Pierre, Bar-sur-Aube

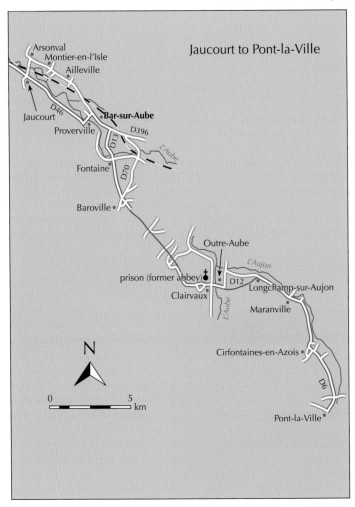

Jaucourt to Pont-la-Ville

Continue through village (**Route de Jaucourt** becomes **Grande Rue**) then enter the town on **Rue Romagnon**. Turn L into **Rue Pierre Brossolette**, cross the river **Aube** and KSO on **Rue de l'Aube** to the mairie.

2km Bar-sur-Aube (485/460) Pop. 6263, 65m

All facilities. Parish office (PS) at Rue Saint-Pierre 4 bis, Accueil almost everyday, 10.00am–12.00pm and 4.00–7.00pm; pilgrim-only accommodation in the presbytère (whose entrance gates are classified as a historic monument), but try to arrive before 7.00pm (otherwise phone 03.25.27.06.34). Three hotels: **Pomme d'Or, Faubourg de Belfort 79 (03.25.27.09.93); Saint-Pierre, Rue Saint-Pierre 5 (03.26.27.13.58); ***Saint-Nicholas, Rue du Général de Gaulle 2 (03.26.27.08.65). TO in Place de l'Hôtel de Ville (03.25.27.24.25).

Eglise Saint-Pierre, second half of 12th century, has a *halloy* (wooden verandah-type porch dating from the 16th century and used for market stalls at fair times) along the south and west sides of the church, originally an *aître* (a type of shelter/cemetery); note the *mesure matrice* in wall – a measure for corn and other cereals dating from about 1570 and which served as a check in case of disputes between buyer and seller. Eglise Saint-Maclou, Chapelle Saint-Jean (former Chapelle des Hospitaliers), 15th-century remains of Hôpital du Saint-Esprit (Avenue Leclerc), several interesting old houses in the town centre. Stage LXV (Bar, 65) in Sigeric's itinerary.

Mesure matrice *(corn measure), Eglise Saint-Pierre, Bar-sur-Aube*

To continue from the mairie, turn R into **Rue Nationale** and then continue between two public garden. KSO ahead along the **Faubourg de Belfort** (Hôtel de la Pomme d'Or on R, at start). Turn R into **Rue Louis Desprez** (not marked, but this is the D13) and KSO to

2km Fontaine (487/458)

Bar/resto.

Looking down over Baroville

Cross the river **Aube** then KSO ahead at junction on **Rue de la Côte d Aube**, cross another branch of the **Aube**, then turn L by bar onto **Rue du Marchepied**. Turn R at end (church to L), then at junction with three trees and a seat veer L uphill. KSO then KSO(L) ahead on gravel track at fork 100m after wayside cross, then KSO ahead when tarred road joins from back R. KSO uphill.

KSO, ignoring turnings, through vines. At top of hill your route is laid out before you like a map, so you can see where you are going next. Go downhill to church and mairie in

2km Baroville (489/456) Pop. 337
CH at Les Combelles (03.25.27.00.36). Tap by mairie.

KSO ahead past church on **Rue des Pressoirs** then **Rue de la Côte Sandrey**. At end continue straight ahead, steeply uphill on rough track, then KSO ahead at top at crossing with wayside cross. 200–300m later fork L onto track (two isolated trees at start) leading through fields to woods ahead. KSO, ignoring turnings, then shortly before you start to enter the woods KSO(L) ahead at fork then KSO, quite literally, on grassy track.

At bottom of the hill a bigger track joins from back L, after which the route is known as **Sommière des Moines**, with woods to either side (and so shady in parts).

1km later reach minor road with hunting club building to L, then KSO ahead on wide gravel track through woods (boggy, even in summer), gradually downhill. When track veers sharp L 500m later KSO ahead, then 500m after that join first a track coming from back L then a minor road coming from back R.

Be careful here. Fork (but not turn) R here, veering R. *(If you do KSO(L) ahead here you will eventually reach the D396 1.5km short (ie north) of Clairvaux; in this case turn R along the main road to the junction in Clairvaux.)*

Reach junction with D101 (this is where the **Sommière des Moines** stops – *bicycles can turn R here, on slightly longer but direct route to abbey*) and turn L, veering R round perimeter walls of former Abbaye de Clairvaux (now a very high-security prison). At end road is joined from behind by the D12 in

8km Clairvaux (497/448)

Bar-tabac at junction by abbey. The nuns of the Fraternité Saint Bernard, Rue de l'Abbaye 14–15, put up families visiting prisoners and are always willing to take pilgrims when space is available, but it is **essential** to phone ahead: 03.25.27.93.31 or 03.25.27.86.48. Small charge, 21 places, self-catering K, PS. Hotel/resto/tabac de l'Abbaye, 600m away at junction with D396 (03.25.27.80.12). Hostellerie des Dames in abbey compound has hotel-type accommodation.

Cistercian abbey founded in 1115 by Saint Bernard. Hostellerie des Dames in abbey compound with small museum – ask here for guided tours of the abbey (afternoons).

Cross D396 and enter hamlet of **Outre Aube** (0.5km) then continue on D12, which does a sharp LH bend 700–800m later. KSO ahead here, uphill on a clear unsurfaced road, and KSO ahead, ignoring turnings. Enter village on **Rue de la Loire** at junction by church in

3km Longchamp-sur-Aujon (500/445) Pop. 450

Seats in shade at entry.

Turn R onto **Rue de Maranville** and KSO to

3km Maranville (503/442) Pop. 49

You are now in the départment of the Haute Marne (52).

Continue through village on main street (D6) and KSO to

3km Cirfontaines-en-Azois (506/439)

Sitting area on R near entrance.

KSO ahead to

3.5km Pont-la-Ville (509.5/435.5) Pop. 151

Shady seat by cemetery (has tap) near entrance.

Continue through village, KSO at crossroads on **Rue de la Motte** (seats opposite church). KSO, cross motorway and KSO on D207. 2km after that turn L into **Marmesse**, veering L by small lake, then turn R at junction by wayside cross. Continue to church, pass to L of it, cross bridge over the **Anjou** (note lavoir to L), veering R. KSO. *(Just before the level crossing the church in Chateauvillain appears framed between buildings ahead.)* Cross railway line, veer R and enter town by junction with D65. KSO ahead on **Rue de Chaumont**, and KSO(L) into **Rue de Penthièvre** to junction with **Rue du Parc** (TO to L in tower in town walls) in

6.5km Châteauvillain (516/471) Pop. 1752, 235m

Shops, etc, TO, Tour de l'Auditoire (15/6–16/9). There is a small pilgrim-only gîte in the town centre (access via TO, 03.25.32.99.22 or 06.88.56.67.94), but otherwise there is no campsite or any other accommodation apart from a CH (also in the town centre), 13 Rue de Penthièvre (Steve and Maggie Tait, 8 places, 03.25.32.08.45 or 06.66.85.08.45).

Châteauvillain, a fortified town at a bend in the river Aujon, may seem a rather 'dead' modern town, but it has a lot of medieval interest and a maze of alleys and parapets. Twenty of the original 60 towers from the 2.6km of

12th–14th-century fortifications surrounding the town are still standing, as are its three gates – the Porte Saint-Jacques, the Porte Madame and one other. Châteauvillain also has the second biggest dovecote in France, with spaces for 3000 birds. (The linguistically curious pilgrim may wonder why there are two words for 'dovecote' in French – *colombier* was the pre-Revolutionary, *pigeonnier* the post-Revolution term). The Parc aux Daims (272 hectares) has more than 100 deer roaming about freely. Châteauvillain has the only lavoir in France with adjustable flooring, a *plancher flottant*. Eglise Notre-Dame, 14th–18th centuries, Chapelle de la Trinité (1604). 18th-century hôtel de ville.

Châteauvillain

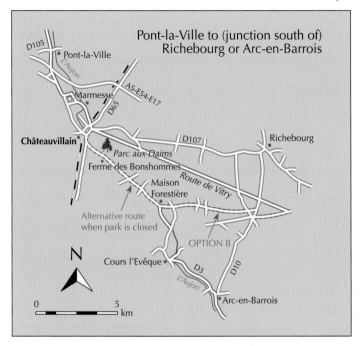

Pont-la-Ville to (junction south of) Richebourg or Arc-en-Barrois

For shops and other facilities continue down **Rue de Penethièvre** and then retrace your steps.

Note *Before you leave Châteauvillain read through the route description as far as Langres. Accommodation is very difficult in this section and two routes are described here, Options A and B (2km longer). Make sure you have food and water with you on this next stretch, especially if you choose Option B.*

To continue (except during the fortnight at the end of October/early November when the park is closed for the deer-breeding season ▼) turn L along **Rue du Parc** (or turn R if you have come from the church) and go past the TO to the **Porte Madame** (the original gateway to the town, dating from the 14th century). *Park open 8.00am–8.00pm (1/5–31/10) and 8.00am–6.00pm (1/11–30/4), except during the deer-breeding season.*

Go through the **Porte Madame** into the **Parc aux Daims** (no bikes or horses allowed), and then turn R onto a very clear gravel (not grass) track ahead. At fork 500m later KSO(L) ahead. KSO, ignoring turnings, until you reach the **Centre**

141

Equestre, and then go through the gates and then the big **Porte des Bonshommes** onto a minor road – the **Ferme des Bonshommes** opposite was formerly a pilgrim halt.

Turn L, cross small bridge then, at bend, KSO(L) ahead into woods on earth track uphill. 150m later road rejoins from back R (ie path was a short-cut). KSO here, and path becomes a very clear gravel track. Continue, ignoring turnings, for 3.5km until you reach a crossing with a deserted stone farmhouse and outbuildings on L, the **Maison Forestière**.

For an **alternative route** out of Châteauvillain during the deer-breeding season continue to church then turn R down Rue Saint-Jaques, then turn L near roundabout into Rue du Collège (back entrance to large supermarket on R). Turn L at fork, marked 'Centre Equestre', continuing past the Ferme des Bonshommes (formerly a pilgrim halt in centuries gone by), and KSO alongside perimeter wall of the Parc aux Daims, a very large deer park.

KSO on wide forest road, with dense woods to either side – the route known as the **Chemin des Bonshommes**. 4km later reach the

6km Maison Forestière (522/423)

At this point there are two options.

OPTION A

Turn R here, veering gradually L. When you reach the edge of the woods KSO ahead at junction, across field to more woods. KSO until you reach the D3 at the entrance to

4km Cours l'Evêque (526/419)

Turn L along road and KSO for 3.5km to

4km Arc-en-Barrois (530/415)

Campsite at entrance (03.25.02.51.33), superette next to TO, bakery, pharmacy, bar/resto, bank and CD. Hôtel du Parc (Logis de France (03.25.02.53.07), CH (03.25.02.50.77). TO (03.25.02.52.17).

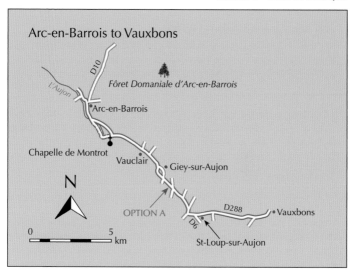

Arc-en-Barrois to Vauxbons

Fôret Domaniale d'Arc-en-Barrois

Arc-en-Barrois

Chapelle de Montrot

Vauclair

Giey-sur-Aujon

N

OPTION A

D288

Vauxbons

St-Loup-sur-Aujon

0   5
╠══════╣ km

Enter village, passing cemetery (on L) and campsite (on R), continue ahead and turn second R on **Rue Abel Pouillain** (the D6, marked 'Giey-sur-Aujon').

1.5km later you can do a small detour if you wish (500m in all) to visit the **Chapelle de Montrot**. If so, fork L onto D259 (CH at corner, 03.25.02.50.77), go through village, veering L and then return to road. Otherwise – simply KSO on D6.

Pass turning to Domaine du Val Bruant (on L). (CH 250m uphill, 03.25.01.57.71.) KSO to entrance to

7km Giey-sur-Aujon (537/408)

Bakery/épicerie/café.

Cross the river **Aujon** (sitting area) and KSO through village, passing two lavoirs (both with covered seating), then veer L by mairie and public garden along **Rue de la Porcelaine**. KSO, uphill, to junction in the centre of

3km Saint-Loup-sur-Aujon (540/405)

Auberge. Pilgrim-only accommodation provided by the Bénédictines de Jésus Christ, Rue du Couvent 1 (essential to phone ahead: 03.25.90.70.68, 5 rooms, 4–6 beds, 1 single). Vespers, compline, lauds, etc.

Continue on the D6, but then turn L onto the D288 (markled 'Vauxbons'), crossing the river. Follow the road round (another joins from back R 500m before village) and reach junction by lavoir in

5km Vauxbons (545/400)

Turn L on **Rue Basse** (D288, marked 'Ormancey'), veering R by war memorial and L at junction by second lavoir, uphill. At junction at top turn R onto C4 (marked 'Voisins'), then 100m later, when this bends sharp R, KSO(L) ahead. 700m later road does a sharp 'kink' to R and then turns hard L, after which it becomes unsurfaced. You can, however (but not bicycles), KSO ahead at bend, down shady grassy lane for 300m (ie short-cut) and then turn L at the bottom to continue.

KSO for 800m more to junction with D143. Turn L then 50m later turn R onto C3 ('Mardor, 1.4km') and continue uphill into

4km Mardor (549/396)

Continue through village on **Rue de Langres** and then out the other side on the C2 ('Saint-Ciergues'). 1.5km later cross motorway and continue on other side. Some 500m later look out for Langres cathedral towers on the skyline to R ahead. KSO to

3.5km St-Ciergues (562.5/362.5)

Eglise St-Cyr et Ste-Juliette, 16th century. Bar/resto Auberge du Lac by lake.

At junction by wayside cross KSO on Rue Saint-Cyr (D28, 'Langres') and continue downhill through village, passing lavoir (L). Turn R at the bottom on **Rue du Lac** (auberge to R, just after dam) then almost immediately turn L down waymarked FP and turn L over the *barrage* (dam – the lake is the **Reservoir de la Mouche**). Turn L on other side (marked 'Fontaine du Bassin') and KSO, passing two LH turns, the second of which is where the Option B, via Mormont and Saint-Martin-lès-Langres, joins up. KSO, veering R uphill, through hamlet of **La Fontaine au Bassin** onto plateau, reaching a wayside cross at the top with good views and Langres on the horizon.

2km later reach junction with D135 and turn L and KSO along it. At junction with wayside cross at entrance to town (*bicycles should continue on the road from here into Langres as the walkers' route is unsuitable*) turn R along **Rue de la Parcheminerie** (C6), passing covered area with seats (former lavoir) on R, to the

5.5km Eglise Notre-Dame de Brévoines (568/377)

Turn to page 147 to continue.

OPTION B

When you reach the **Maison Forestière** (on L) KSO(L) ahead. 3km after that reach a crossing with another forest track (picnic tables and covered rest area to R), and 3km later reach the D10 and turn L.

CH at Richebourg and, 3km further on, Thérèse and Patrick Devilliers, 23 Domaine d'Orchamps (03.25.31.05.46, la.maison.renaud@wanadoo.fr), just north of village.

Otherwise (having turned L), take the second turning on the R onto a forest road, veering L at end to the D102. Turn R, passing **Ferme du Val des Dames** (on L) and KSO through fields, leaving forest, to hamlet of

12km Mormant

Ancienne Abbaye (by wayside cross, visits possible). CH Mme Michelet, Rue de l'Abbaye 14 (03.25.31.21.41).

Follow the D102 round (marked 'Leffonds'), cross motorway and KSO, passing three wayside crosses, to

3km Leffonds, Pop. 285, 380m

PO.

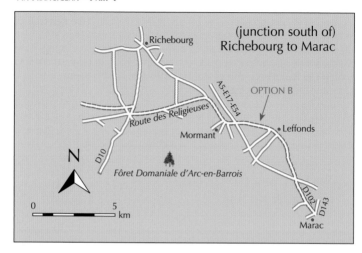

Continue ahead on D102 (marked 'Leffonds Centre'), downhill, veering R on **Rue des Côtes** and then uphill (**Chemin des Fontaines**) to junction and turn L to church. Turn R (seats) into **Rue de la Cressonière** shortly afterwards at junction. Go under motorway and KSO ahead to

6km Marac, Pop. 173, 370m
14th-century château.

Continue ahead through village (**Rue de Bourgogne**) to junction by war memorial (*there are seats behind and a historic dovecote, signposted 'Colombier' just behind Salle des Fêtes*). Turn L (**Rue des Charmes** – note lavoir on L), crossing bridge over small river. KSO uphill to fork by wayside cross and KSO(R) ahead.

3km later join D3 coming from back R and cross motorway. KSO to

4.5km Beauchemin
No facilities. Parish office may be able to find you accommodation, but they are based in Rolamport, not here, so you will need to phone ahead (03.25.84.72.69).

Dovecote in Marac

At second junction fork R onto C5. 1.5km later KSO(L) at fork. Road veers sharp R (turn L here for church and rejoin D286 in village) to T-junction with D286 and turn L (fork L immediately afterwards on one-way street for short-cut to middle of village) into

2.5km Saint-Martin-lès-Langres, Pop. 54

Continue on main street past lavoir (L), then at junction turn hard R downhill on C3, zigzagging down to Moulin Saint-Martin. Cross river and then another bridge, veering L on other side to T-junction with C1. *This is where Option A, via Arc-en-Barrois and Saint-Ciergues, joins up with Option B.* Turn L then, 150m later, KSO(R) ahead at another junction, uphill, through hamlet of **La Fontaine au Bassin** and up onto plateau.

2km later reach junction with D135 and turn L and KSO along it. At junction with wayside cross at entrance to town (*bicycles should continue on the road from here into Langres as the walkers' route is unsuitable*) turn R along **Rue de la Parcheminerie** (C6), passing covered area with seats (former lavoir) on R, to the

10km Eglise Notre-Dame de Brévoines

Church dating from 12th century, originally dedicated to Saint-Renobert (patron saint of domestic animals), restored 2003 and worth visiting as it contains several listed 16th- and 17th-century polychrome statues (both wood and stone).

Both routes Turn L (**Rue Chanoine Charles F Roussel**), cross river (**La Bonnelle**) and continue ahead uphill (becomes shady). *The church tower you can see on the skyline is the Eglise Saint-Martin (of which there are some 2999 more in France!).*

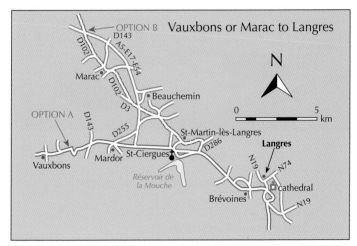

Approaching Langres

The road does a sharp bend to L, then you cross the bridge over a 'Voie Verte' ('Greenway'), a cycle track, and turn R on other side, veering L uphill on **Rue des Sources** (wayside cross part way up and shady seat on L near top).

Reach a bigger road (**La Belle Allée**) running parallel to the ramparts above you, go up steps, cross over, and on other side go up more steps by fountain, veering R up to small door, then on other side turn L through **Porte de l'Hôtel de Ville** to **Place de l'Hôtel de Ville** in

2km Langres (570/375) Pop. 9586, 475m

All facilities. SNCF, YH in FJT (Foyer des Jeunes Travailleurs), Place des Etats-Unis (in upper town, 03.25.86.09.69 or 03.25.86.76.74; you can sleep there every day, including Sat and Sun nights, but can not book in on Sat pm or all day Sun). Camping Navarre (Bd de Lattre de Tassigny, 03.25.87.37.92). Hôtel-Restaurant La Marmotte, Avenue Général de Gaulle (03.25.87.53.24), *Hôtel Le Moulins, Place des Etats-Unis (03.25.87.08.12), **Hôtel de la Poste, Place Ziegler 8–10 (03.25.87.10.51), Grand Hôtel de l'Europe, Rue Diderot 23–25 (03.25.87.10.88). TO Square Olivier-Lahalle (Place Bel'Air, 03.25.87.60.62, info@tourisme-langres.com).

Gallo-Roman fortified town with ramparts and several extant town gates, built on a promontory looking out over the whole area. Birthplace of Diderot (square named after him has the house where he was born – 6 – and also 9, where his family lived). Cathédrale de Saint-Mammes (the present building dates from the mid-12th century), with ambulatory permitting pilgrims to walk round behind the high altar and view the saint's relics. Eglise Saint-Martin (13th and 16th centuries), Musée d'Art et Histoire. The region, in general, is famous for its wickerwork and cutlery manufacture.

'Raising of Lazarus', polychrome sculpture scene, Langres cathedral

To continue (from the **Place de l'Hôtel de Ville**), cross square diagonally R and go up **Rue Charles Beligné**, then turn second L up **Rue St-Didier** to **Place Jeanne Mancé** (named after the co-founder of Montréal, Quebec) to the cathedral.

Turn R (facing the cathedral) along **Rue du Général Leclerc**, then continue to **Place Diderot**, **Rue Diderot**, **Place du Théâtre** and **Place Colonel de Grouchy** to **Place des Etats Unis** and TO.

To continue KSO ahead along **Avenue Turenne**, then enter **Citadelle** and KSO ahead along **Avenue du 21ième Regiment d'Infanterie**. Leave Citadelle and reach a roundabout. Continue to second roundabout and fork L onto D122. KSO for 2.5km then turn L onto D290 (marked 'Balesmes-sur-Marne' and 'Source de la Marne'). Pass turning to 'Source de la Marne' (with two tracks coming from L on other side of D290). KSO ahead, downhill to

7km Balesmes-sur-Marne (577/368) Pop. 260

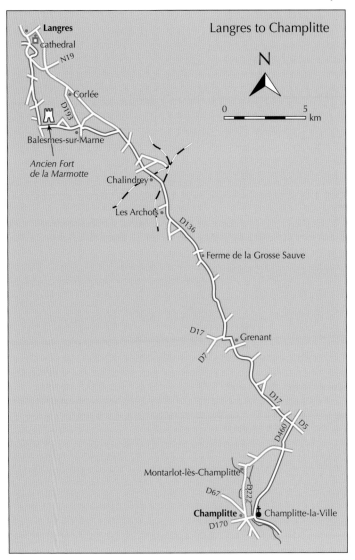

Langres to Champlitte

N

0 — 5 km

Langres

cathedral

N19

Corlée

D193

Balesmes-sur-Marne

Ancien Fort
de la Marmotte

Chalindrey

Les Archots

D136

Ferme de la Grosse Sauve

D17

Grenant

D7

D17

D460   D5

Montarlot-lès-Champlitte

D222

D67

Champlitte   Champlitte-la-Ville

D170

At first junction (water tower and wayside cross) KSO(R) ahead. At next junction turn L (**Rue de l'Eglise**) then KSO (**Rue de Saint-Mole**), cross the river **Marne** (only a mere trickle in summer), and then KSO on D290 for 3km more to D17. Turn R and KSO for 3km more to

6km Chalindrey (583/362) Pop. 270, 350m

Shops, etc, SNCF, bakery, Auberge de la Gare (hotel/bar/resto), bar/tabac by church, bakery, superette.

At junction (D17 turns R here) KSO ahead on D136. Cross railway line (twice), and 4km later either turn R to **Les Archots** (to sleep in Gîte François and CH, 03.25.88.93.64, 700m west, on L, before bridge over the river) or KSO on D136 to continue.

KSO on D136. Pass **Ferme de la Grosse Sauve**, former pilgrim halt. KSO, woods most of the way. At junction with D7 KSO(L) ahead for 1.5km to

10km Grenant (593/352)

Stage LXII (Grenant, 62) in Sigeric's itinerary. (Stages LXIV (Blaecuile, 64) and LXIII (Oisma, 63) were, respectively, in Blessonville and Humes, off the route of the Via Francigena as described in this guide.)

KSO through village, cross the river **Salon** (seat on other side, near church) and continue. Veer L past church and then at cross roads turn L uphill on D17 (**Rue de Frette**). Partly shaded. KSO.

When you leave the département of the Haute Marne (52) and enter the Haute Saône (70) (leaving the Champagne region behind and entering Franche-Comté), the road then becomes the D5.

The Franche-Comté is noted for its clochers comtois (or clochers à l'impériale), of which there are more than 700 still in existence. These are church towers, usually dome-shaped, and covered in multi-coloured enamelled tiles. Each one is slightly different, although there are some recurrent features, such as the criss-cross layout in the design of many of them. The region is also characterised by its many lavoirs (outdoor communal facilities for washing clothes), worthy of note by pilgrims interested in vernacular architecture.

After 6km (from Grenant) reach crossing with the D460 and turn R. KSO and 7km later enter

13km Champlitte (606/339) Pop. 1900, 240m

Shops, banks, etc. Gîte communal (contact mairie: 0384.67.64.10), gîte rural (contact mairie, 03.83.67.64.10 or 03.84.67.69.57). **Hôtel-Restaurant du Donjon, Rue de la République 46 (03.84.67.66.95), Camping Municipal, Route de Leffonds. TO (03.84.67.67.19).

Old fortified camp town founded in the 10th century and strategically placed on a promontory overlooking the ford over the river Salon, the Roman road linking Langres with Besançon (a trade route) and the boundaries of three provinces – Burgundy, Champagne and the Franche-Comté. Its 18th-century castle (visits possible) now houses a regional museum of folk art and customs and two other museums. Eglise Saint-Christophe (rebuilt 1818) has original 14th-century tower. The town had four monasteries in former times and a royal hospital. The TO has a leaflet with a plan for a 30min walking tour of the town, which will give you an idea of what it used to be like in the past.

Turn L at junction with **Rue des Casernes** (that you entered on) into **Route de Champlitte la Ville**. However, to visit the church, mairie, TO, shop, hotel and other bar (all these are up on the main road) turn R up **Rue Pasteur** and **Rue du Bourg** and R along **Rue de la République**.

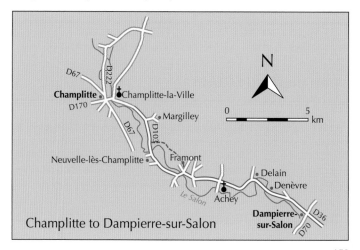

Champlitte to Dampierre-sur-Salon

Street in Champlitte

1km Champlitte-la-Ville (607/338)

Eglise Saint-Christophe (listed building) worth a visit. 11th-century octagonal baptismal font with very clear symbolic designs. To visit (if not open): 03.84.67.66.26 or 03.84.67.65.12.

Continue through village, veering R by church (seats nearby) – note patterned tiles on its roof – and then veer L on D103 (**Route de Margilley**). KSO to

1.5km Margilley (608.5/336.5)

Continue through village and then turn R by church (C2) onto **Route de Neuvelle**. 1.5km later look out for the waymarks of the GRP Châteaux et Villages de Haute-Sâone, which leaves the road to the L and goes directly to Framont. *(From there it wends its way via Montot to pass (but not enter) Dampierre-sur-Salon.)* Otherwise KSO for 2km, cross river (**Le Salon**) and turn L at junction into

2km Neuvelle-lès-Champlitte (610.5/334.5)

KSO on D36 to

2km Framont (612.5/332.5)

Cross bridge over **Le Salon** (sitting area on R after bridge) and continue ahead on **Grande Rue**, veering R past lower church. At bend 200m later KSO(R) ahead on **Rue de la Cure**, veering L and then R to upper church (to R) and **Place de l'Eglise**. Continue ahead on D36 (**Rue de Dampierre**, but not marked at start).

2km Achey (614.5/330.5)

Continue through village on D36 to

2.5km Delain (617/328)

Church has statue of Saint Peter inside, with keys, cockerel and roll (of paper).

Continue through village, veer R by lavoir and KSO past church. Cross **Le Salon** again and KSO to

1km Denèvre (618/327)

CH Rue de Fouvent on entry.

Continue on D36 to end of village, veering L near river. KSO for 3km, entering town via **Rue de Champlitte**.

Saint Peter, Delain church

3km Dampierre-sur-Salon (621/324)

2 bakeries, CH La Tour des Moines, 7 rue de Fouvent (Odette and Bernard Monney, 03.84.67.16.37 or 06.30.47.86.64), Centre de Loisirs Croq'Loisirs (mairie, 03.84.67.14.30).

Late 18th-century Eglise Notre-Dame de la Nativité, built on the site of the former Eglise Saint-Pierre. Mairie-lavoir, a feature found in other places in this area too; this particular building has the municipal offices on the first floor and is built over the river, with the washing area underneath, and open to the public.

Continue ahead on **Rue Louis Dornier**, passing large supermarket on R and then, at junction, KSO on D36 (marked 'Seveux'). *This was Stage LXI (61, Sefui) in Sigeric's itinerary, but is off the route described here.*
After 3.5km fork R on D172 to

6km Savoyeux (627/318)

Stay on D172, veering R. Cross bridge over the Saône and reach

2km Mercey-sur-Saône (629/316)

CH Rue Château (03.84.67.07.84).

To enter village turn R. To continue turn L (D172) alongside the river to

2km Motey-sur-Saône (631/314)

Turn R at junction in village onto D13, then 400m later turn L onto D174. KSO, mainly through forest, to small hamlet of

3.5km Sainte-Reine (634.5/310.5)

Dampierre-sur-Salon to Oiselay-et-Grachaux

Follow road round through village, KSO at crossing with D175 (marked 'Igny'), pass mairie (R) and then, when D174 bends L at road KM 1, KSO ahead (signed 'sauf riverains'). Veer L at bend and 1.5km after leaving Sainte-Reine reach the D5. Turn R along it for 2km to

4.5km La Chapelle Saint-Quillon (639/306)

Large village green with shady picnic area and fountain near church. Lavoir with covered seating. Campsite signposted to L. The church contains a 16th-century statue of the Irish Saint Quillan.

Continue for a short distance past church on D5, then turn L onto minor road marked 'La Montbleuse', mainly through forest, to hamlet of

3km La Montbleuse (642/303)

Turn R at crossroads then L on another minor road (marked 'Frasne-le-Château'). KSO to

3km Frasne-le-Château (645/300) Pop. 180

Foyer des Jeunes Travailleurs (03.84.32.48.05).

On leaving the village head for the D474, but make sure you leave by the D394, as the road you need on the opposite side of the D474 isn't marked. On the other side there are two minor roads plus a turning area for vehicles going east that want to turn L into Frasne-le-Château. Take the second (RH) road (this is the C1, although it isn't marked), leaving diagonally to R away from main road. KSO for 3km more, passing kennels and a cattery plus **Centre Canin Balzac** (dog-training school) on R and reach

4km Grachaux (649/296)

KSO through village and KSO(L) at junction with bus shelter. After 1.5km reach D5 coming from back R and continue on it to

5km Oiselay-et-Grachaux (654/291) Pop. 381

Bar/pizzeria.

KSO along D5 through village to

3.5km Bonnevent-Velloreille (657.5/287.5) Pop. 287

A very long, straggling village.

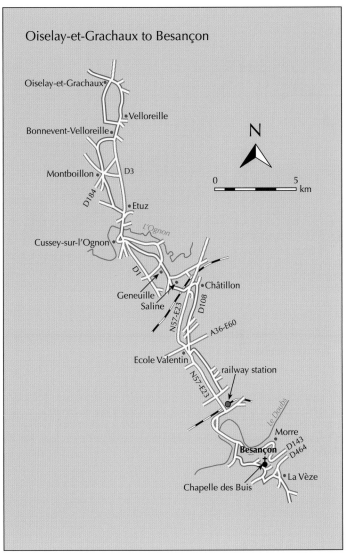

Oiselay-et-Grachaux to Besançon

Farmhouse in Montboillon

Continue on D5 for 1.5km then turn R onto D194 to

3km Montboillon (660.5/284.5)

Continue down to junction by mairie, veering L on D194 marked 'Gézier'. Go uphill, then just before road bends R, turn L down **Rue du Trembois**, a ridge route with good views, which becomes a track after a while. Follow it downhill to T-junction with minor road then turn L there, uphill and then down **Rue du Moulin** to D3 and centre of

3km Etuz (663.5/281.5) Pop. 564
Tabac/presse (and food supplies).

Turn R on **Grande Rue** (note lavoir to L) and KSO on D3 to

1.5km Cussey-sur-l'Ognon (665/280) Pop. 62

Shop opposite mairie, ***Hotel Vieille Auberge by church (03.81.48.51.70) and Hôtel Chez la Marie (has PS) at bend on road afterwards (03.81.57.78.32). Stage LX (60, Cuscei) in Sigeric's itinerary.

Cross over the river **L'Ognon**, and at church KSO ahead past shop on **Rue du Village**. At top of hill turn L into **Rue du Château**, and then R on **Rue des Ballotes**. Road becomes a track. Veer L by house then pass to L of wooden building, veering R on FP through woods. Follow it round then, when houses start, KSO ahead down hill (**Chemin du Vauveret**), veering R onto **Rue de la Gratotte**, veering L to the church in

5km Geneuille (670/275)

Bar/resto/tabac/presse, bakery. CH Rue de l'Abreuvoir 18 (03.81.55.68.99).

Turn R in front of church then KSO ahead at junction in village, passing café/ tabac (on L). KSO(R) ahead at roundabout (D14, 'Besançon'), then 250m later, when road bends R, KSO(L) ahead to small village of **Saline** (1km), go over level crossing and continue ahead to N57. Turn R onto it and then immediately L onto a forest track that veers R to run more or less parallel to main road. Follow it uphill (it becomes a road when houses start) to the D108 in **Les Rancenières** (a *lieu-dit*, locality) and turn R along it.

KSO for 2km, reach a roundabout, then KSO ahead on **Route de Chatillon**, on cycle track/pavement through area with a lot of large rocks (cafeteria on L). Cross the motorway and continue to a roundabout by a petrol station. KSO ahead (marked 'Valentin') and enter

8km Ecole Valentin (678/267)

You are also on a bus route to the centre of Besançon here, in case you are very tired or it is getting late.

KSO(L) ahead on Rue de la Combe du Puits, veering L uphill, then turn R (still the **Rue de la Combe du Puits**), which becomes the **Chemin de Valentin** at the

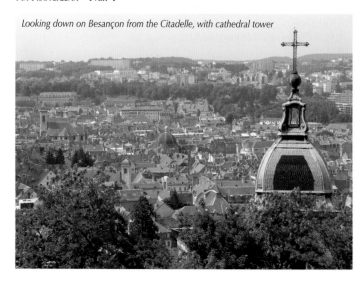

Looking down on Besançon from the Citadelle, with cathedral tower

junction with the **Rue Champêtre**, where you enter the city of Besançon (although you will have to turn round to see the sign, as it is only indicated coming from the other direction). At a small roundabout at the bottom of the hill KSO, but then watch out for the LH turn uphill on **Chemin des Torcols**, veering R.

Note The description that follows may differ slightly from the waymarked route.

KSO at roundabout (still the **Chemin des Torcols**), then at next roundabout KSO ahead on **Rue Francis Clerc**, a long street. At the very end the Rue Francis Clerc becomes **Rue Henri Baigne**.

If you want to sleep in the FJT/YH Foyer des Oiseaux, 48 Rue des Cras (03.81.40.32.02), turn L here towards a church, veering R, then turn L into Rue du Chasnot, then KSO ahead along Rue Trémolières and Rue Prof. George into Rue des Cras.

Otherwise, veer R into **Rue Nicolas Bruand**, cross the railway line then turn L immediately. At end turn R (still **Rue Nicolas Bruand**), with the railway line to the L. At end turn L into **Rue de Vesoul** to pass under the railway lines. Veer L on other side along **Avenue de la Paix** towards the railway station, but do not go under the road bridge. When you get level with the station turn R onto pavement of main road and go down a flight of steps to the underpass to turn R, emerging in a park on the other side.

KSO ahead, slightly downhill, veering L, to then turn R over pedestrian bridge over the N83. KSO ahead on other side (another park) towards the **Tour Carrée** (a stone tower), then pass to R of it and go down steps and path leading downhill to the **Tour de la Pelote**, now a restaurant.

Turn L at the bottom along the **Quai de Strasbourg** and then turn R over the **Pont Denfert Rochereau**.

However, to visit the TO (eg to collect a street plan) KSO ahead along lower-level path alongside the river Doubs (access it before crossing the bridge), to the R of the Avenue d'Hélvétie above you, alongside river. Go under next bridge (Pont de la République) then turn hard L to TO, in a modern building above you. Then retrace your steps (or return on upper level path) and turn left over Pont Denfert Rochereau.

To continue, fork R on other side down **Rue Gustave Courbet** to the **Place de la Révolution** and then turn L into the **Rue des Granges**. Turn second R into the **Rue de la République**, veering L in front of the **Eglise Saint-Pierre** and then L into the **Grande Rue**. KSO to the very end, then continue ahead on **Rue de la Convention**, passing **Square Castan** (to L, with remains of semi-circular Roman theatre) and **Arcier acqueduct** (site of original Eglise Saint-Jean) and go under archway (**Porte Noire**) to the **Cathédrale Saint-Jean** in

---

6km Besançon (684/261) Pop. 125,000

Large town with all facilities. SNCF. Accommodation in all price brackets, including Foyer des Jeunes Travailleurs/YH (Foyer des Oiseaux), Rue des Cras 48 (03.81.40.32.02), another FJT (La Cassotte, 03.81.51.98.68), CIS (Centre International de Séjour), Avenue des Montboucons (03.81.50.07.54), Monastère de Sainte-Claire, Rue du Chapître 5 (03.81.82.10.25) and L'Escale-Jeunes (03.81.81.21.11). TO 2 Place de la 1ière Armée Française 2 (03.81.80.92.55, info@besançon-tourisme.com), PS in cathedral.

Situated in a horseshoe-shaped bend in the river Doubs, Besançon is a good place for a day off and the town has many sights. Cathédrale Saint-Jean, Rue de la Convention, 12th century onwards, is unusual in having two apses but no main façade (the entrance is via an 18th-century side portal). It has the oldest clocher comtois in existence, dating from 1784, and the Rose de Saint-Jean (an 11th-century circular white marble altar), and houses the Horloge Astronomique, assembled in the 19th century with 30,000 moving parts which run 57 faces providing information on calendars, the movement of the planets, eclipses, etc (guided tours available). PS, mass 6.15pm Sundays, preceded by sung vespers at 5.30pm.

The Citadelle was built by Vauban (who built numerous other forts in different parts of France) between 1668 and 1688 on an 11 hectare site, and a walk along its parapets offers impressive views of the city and surrounding area 100m below. Of interest are the bastion Saint-Etienne, the royal façade (built by the Spanish), a well dug 132m (43ft) into the rock and the 16th-century Chapelle Saint-Etienne. The Citadelle also houses three museums – Musée Comtois (regional folk museum), Musée de la Résistance et de la Déportation and the Musée d'Histoire Naturelle.

Besançon's other sights include the Hôpital Saint-Jacques (17th and 18th centuries, housing one of the finest old dispensaries in France, visits available), the Musée des Beaux Arts et d'Archéologie (France's oldest museum), the Musée des Temps (clocks and watches) in the Palais Granvelle, the 16th-century hôtel de ville and the Porte Noire, a triumphal arch built around AD175, during the reign of Marcus Aurelius. Walking around the town the visitor will notice the many decorative fountains, now restored, and the well-preserved Renaissance buildings constructed in yellow-ochre-coloured stone shot through with steel-blue seams. Stage LIX (59, Bysiceon) in Sigeric's itinerary.

To visit the Citadelle ▼ (there is also a regular shuttle bus service (*navette*) from Chamars to the Citadelle), go up flight of steps to L of main door of cathedral then go up **Rue des Fusillés de la Résistance** and at first 'hairpin' continue on FP, zigzagging uphill to the Citadelle.

To continue the route without visiting the Citadelle, turn R in front of the cathedral along **Rue du Chapitre**, veer L past **Monastère Sainte-Claire** on **Rue de la Vieille Monnaie** and then go down steps to emerge by the **Gendarmerie** at the start of **Faubourg Tarragnoz**. Turn L along it and then continue as described in Section 5.

BESANÇON TO LAUSANNE

Leaving Besançon on Chemin de la Petite Creuse

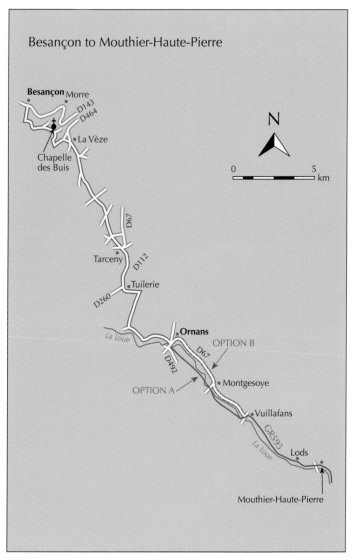

Besançon to Mouthier-Haute-Pierre

SECTION 5
Besançon to Lausanne (135km)

To leave Besançon after visiting the Citadelle, you can either retrace your steps to the cathedral or turn L on leaving entrance hall and then turn L at bend down FP marked 'Tarragnoz'. Continue downhill and then on lengthy stone staircase in sections (not recommended in wet weather with a heavy rucksack), finally emerging by the **Gendarmerie** building at the start of **Faubourg Tarragnoz** (a street). Turn L along it to continue and leave Besançon.

KSO along **Faubourg Tarragnoz** (towpath possible) by river, pass the **Passarelle de Mazagram** (a footbridge) and when the road divides turn hard L uphill, up the **Chemin de la Petite Creuse**, a FP that becomes a staircase. Turn L at the top onto a road (**Chemin de Malpas**), then at junction turn hard R (**Chemin de Trois Chastels**). At junction at top turn L (**Chemin de la Chapelle des Buis**) then at bend with crash barrier (chapel visible on skyline) KSO(R) ahead between houses No 18 and No 22, uphill on grassy walled lane, then steps. This section is waymarked, but not very systematically. Cross a track, continue on stony FP on other side, cross another track, continue on narrow FP then turn L along next track to road (all these are short-cuts). Turn R and continue uphill, zigzagging (stations of the cross en route) up to the

5km Chapelle des Buis (690/255)

Chapel very simple inside. Pilgrim venue in its own right. Good views over Besançon on a clear day. Pilgrim accommodation possible in the Ermitage (03.81.81.33.25).

The waymarked route tells you to continue past church then turn L, veering R, to visit the Monument de la Libération. Be careful, though, as the waymarking is insuffficient at present, and if you follow the GR59 you will end up in Morre, too far over to the east.

Instead continue ahead past chapel on **Route de la Chapelle des Buis** (which then becomes the D144, Route des Buis). Then turn R onto **Chemin de Fontaine** (D143), continue for 1km to D104, turn L and then 800m later fork R marked 'La Vèze'. KSO and turn R into **Rue des Lilas** and then R into **Grande Rue**. Continue ahead on **Rue de l'Ecole**, downhill, into

3km La Vèze (693/252)

Bar/resto Le Vezois on R.

Continue ahead on **Grande Rue** (bar/resto on R). KSO ahead at junction when D246 turns L and KSO. KSO(L) ahead at fork for **La Grande Combe** and go through the *lieux-dits* (localities) of **Le Baraquet** and **La Vieille Baraque**.

At staggered crossing (**Les Fougères**, R) KSO(L) ahead (**Les Cloutiers**) through hamlet/lieu-dit. KSO, pass two large ponds (*étangs*) on R. Cross a more major road at mini-roundabout and KSO ahead on **Rue Sous Velle** uphill into

7km Tarceny (700/245) Pop. 639, 485m

At top of hill join D67 coming from back L and KSO ahead. KSO. Pass **La Tuilerie** (former tile manufacture) and KSO.

At entry to Ornans KSO past roundabout (large supermarket to L) on **Route de Besançon** then **Avenue du Maréchal de Lattre de Tassigny**. KSO ahead at roundabout (**Rond Point de l'Europe**) on **Avenue du Président Wilson** and reach **Place Courbet** in the centre of

9.5km Ornans (709.5/235.5) Pop. 4128, 330m

SCRB. Hôtel de la Vallée, 39 Avenue du Président Wilson 39 (on way into town) (03.81.62.40.43). Hôtel La Table de Gustave, 11 Rue Gervais (opposite PO, 03.81.62.16.79). Gîte Roses et Loue (03.81.57.31.43 or 03.20.79.26.30), Gîte-Camping Le Chanet (03.81.62.23.44). TO Rue Pierre Vernier 7 (03.81.62.21.50) has leaflet with walking circuit to visit town and its many interesting old buildings.

Birthplace of the painter Gustave Courbet (the house is now a museum). Eglise Saint-Laurent, Gothic style, Musée du Costume et des Traditions Comtoises.

OPTION A – THE GR595

To continue on the GR595 Cross the **Loue** by turning R over the **Grand Pont** and then turn L on the other side, following the river Loue all the way to Vuillafans.

OPTION B – THE ROAD

To continue on road From **Place Courbet** KSO on **Rue Pierre Vernier**, **Rue Eugène Cusenier** and **Rue Eduard Basque**, go under viaduct, and then continue (R) ahead

River Loue

on **Route de Montgesoye**, alongside the river **Loue** to start with. This is the D67, but there is a cycle track (as far as Villafans, at least). KSO to

3km Montgesoye (712.5/232.5) Pop. 445, 365m

Camping municipal, Route de la Grange Millet (03.81.62.23.14).

KSO on D67 again to

3km Vuillafans (715.5/229.5) Pop. 677, 354m

Superette, pharmacie, PO. Hotel/resto, 2 other bar/restos. Gîte municipal du Pré Bailly, with campsite (turn R at junction in village, 03.81.60.91.52). Gîte d'étape la Tuffière (turn R at junction opposite church, Chemin de Montgesoye, 03.81.60.96.76). 16th-century church and interesting old houses.

Both routes KSO on D67 to village exit boards then fork L uphill by wayside cross on **Chemin de Croux** (waymarked for GR595 and also in blue and yellow),

Main street, Lods

then fork L again 200m later on **Chemin des Vignes**. Road then becomes a track, up and down, on side of hill, well above road, through vines.

At the end of the rows of Chardonnay grapes look out for a small gateway and turn R downhill, veering L through trees. Continue more or less level along side of hill, parallel to road below for a while, then go through another small gateway and go downhill on steep stony FP, back to the D67 by road KM 56.

Turn L and KSO into

4km Lods (719.5/225.5) Pop. 276, 361m

Shop/bakery. **Hôtel la Truite d'Or (Logis de France), Route de Besançon 40 (at entrance, 03.81.60.95.48), Hôtel de France, Place Pézard 1 (in centre of village by bridge, 03.81.60.95.29): both have restaurants. Camping Le Champaloux (03.81.60.90.11). Musée de la Vigne et du Vin. 18th-century church.

KSO on D67. Campsite at Les Oyes (03.81.60.97.68) and a second, simpler one, shortly afterwards, both by main road.

Continue on road to

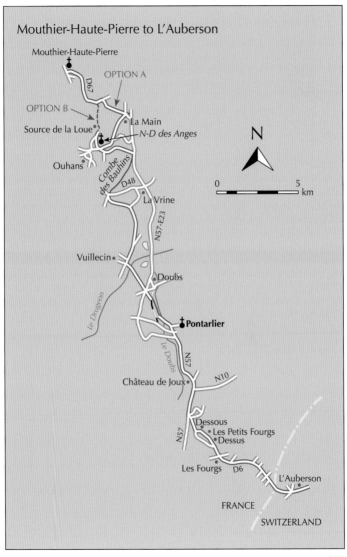

Mouthier-Haute-Pierre to L'Auberson

2.5km Mouthier-Haute-Pierre (722/223) Pop. 349, 450m

Bakery/shop (X Tues), bar/resto by church. Gîte Le Syrah (down by river, 03.81.60.91.10), Gîte Miabollet (above village on the way to Haute Pierre (03.81.60.98.99). ***Hôtel Restaurant La Cascade (03.81.60.95.30). TO (in mairie, 03.81.60.97.68) has book of walks including one for a tour of the village.

Small village originating with a Benedictine priory dating from AD800. Eglise Saint-Laurent (16th century).

After this, as far as Pontarlier, the route is problematic. Because of the hilly nature of the terrain, with gorges with overhanging cliffs and rivers, there are few minor roads, and the N57, that you will get to later, is extremely dangerous to walk on. You have two options – the GR route via the Source de la Loue (Option A), which is shorter, going direct to Ouhans, and a longer route on minor roads (Option B).

OPTION A – ROAD ROUTE

This takes you round two sides of a triangle in order to avoid the N57. Continue uphill on the D67, following it round, uphill all the time, for 6km until you reach the junction with the D41 by a large sawmill (shortly before reaching the N57) in the hamlet of

6km La Main (728/217)

Turn R (marked 'Ouhans 3') and continue downhill. **The Sanctuaire de Notre-Dame des Anges** is visible on hilltop to R ahead, 2km later. Reach junction with D443 at **Le Bas des Traits**, a crossroads 600m to the east of

3km Ouhans (731/214) Pop. 287, 600m

**Hotel/resto/bar Les Sources de la Loue (Logis de France), Grande Rue 13 (03.81.69.90.06). Specialist cheese shop, PO.

To go into Ouhans, KSO ahead for 600m then retrace your steps to continue.

OPTION B – GR ROUTE

This is a spectacular route (and well waymarked) in dry, sunny weather (you don't need to have a good head for heights, but you **do** need to be fairly agile, especially as you will probably be carrying a reasonably heavy rucksack), but it is definitely **not** recommended either in wet weather or if you are alone, as if you slipped and fell nobody would find you very quickly.

Go up the D67 for 1.5km then turn R onto a waymarked track downhill (the route is extremely well waymarked and maintained), zigzagging down to the junction by the **Source du Pontot** (another river). Turn R here and KSO. Cross two metal FBs, and after the second turn L (waterworks building to R). Turn L over wooden FB and KSO, uphill and down, with the **Loue** below you to L, on a clearly marked FP that is sometimes level, sometimes narrow, sometimes wide and often slippery. Some 2hrs later reach the **Source**, with a visitors' centre and explanatory boards.

Continue up track leading to car park, with shop and bar/resto and then continue up the D443 to junction on the edge of **Ouhans** and continue as described below.

Both routes Turn L onto a road marked 'Route forestière sans issue', then turn L 100m later on similar road. KSO, mainly uphill all the time. 1.5km later, in a clearing, with a clear gravel track ahead and a 'parking de chasse' notice, do **not** KSO ahead into pine woods but turn L, steeply uphill (traffic from the N57 audible ahead now). At sharp LH bend shortly afterwards watch out for waymarks indicating a RH turn onto a rough grassy track. This becomes steeper, but clearer as you go. 200m later veer R onto FP leading 100m later to a lay-by at the side of the N57, between road KM 58 and 59. Turn R, and at end of lay-by continue below the road (ie on its RH side) on clear gravel track that runs parallel for a while and then veers off R through the woods – this is the **Chemin des Bauhins**, mainly shady. KSO(R) at fork onto clearer of two options.

The track disintegrates after a while due to tree cutting, but KSO, cross field and re-enter woods, after which the track improves. Go along the edge of two fields, cross another, veering R, and KSO.

3km after the lay-by reach the D48 (notice says 'VF abri 300m' to L) and turn R. 250m later reach junction and turn L. KSO. KSO(R) at fork and KSO again, ignoring turnings to L or R until you reach the church (with clocher comtois) in

10km Vuillecin (741/204) Pop. 548

Turn L here by mairie onto **Rue de Pontarlier**, cross river (**Le Drugeon**) and KSO(R) ahead at fork. KSO.

1km later cross D57 (big roundabout) and KSO ahead on other side, passing to RH side of large supermarket on **Chemin** (and then **Rue**) **Vuillecin**. At next roundabout KSO ahead on **Rue de Besançon** (that joins you from back L, useful street plan at start). KSO(R) at fork and continue to **Place Saint-Pierre** in

5km Pontarlier (746/199) Pop. 18,400, 840m

All facilities. YH, Rue Jouffroy 2 (03.81.39.06.57), Maison Familiale, Rue des Granges 220 (03.81.39.17.04), Cure Saint-Bénigne (03.81.39.00.37 or 06.71.69.73.99). Hotels: **Saint Pierre, Place Saint-Pierre 3 (03.81.46.50.80), **Hôtel/resto du Morteau, Rue Jeanne-d'Arc 26 (03.81.39.14.83), *Bar/ Hôtel de France, Rue de la Gare 8 (03.81.39.05.20). TO Rue de la Gare 14bis (03.81.46.83.32).

Note If you are continuing into Italy after you leave Switzerland, make sure you have enough euros with you for the first two or three days you are there, as before then you will not have the chance to change any money directly, ie without converting it first into Swiss francs, thus incurring two sets

View of Pontarlier,

of charges. (After Pontarlier the next cash machine is in Sainte-Croix, where you can only withdraw Swiss francs.)

Pontarlier was renowned for its absinthe production, a green alcoholic liquid originally developed for medicinal purposes (its chief ingredient was the toxic wormwood shrub) that became so popular as a drink that by the end of the 19th century France's absinthe consumption exceeded 13 million litres a year. Henri Pernod bought the rights to the recipe and opened a distillery in Pontarlier in 1805, but when the drink was officially banned in 1915, on account of its toxicity, he turned to producing an 'imitation' (ie a 'pastiche') instead, omitting the wormwood and producing the aniseed-flavoured aperitif – *pastis* – that is commonly referred nowadays to simply as either a Pernod or a Ricard.

Eglise Saint-Pierre, Musée d'Automobiles, Musée Municipal d'Art et d'Histoire. Stage LVII (Punterlin, 57) in Sigeric's itinerary (LVIII, 58, was in Nods, off the route described here, to the east).

From Place Saint-Pierre KSO ahead along **Rue de la République** (for YH turn second R on **Rue Thiers**, turn L, and it is on **Rue Jouffroy**, second R). Continue along **Faubourg Saint-Etienne** then **Avenue de Neuchâtel**, then **Avenue de l'Armée de l'Est** – all this is the N57 (very noisy), although parts of it have pavement. KSO. Pass war memorial on L and enter **Commune de La Cluse et Mijoux** (made up of several small hamlets/villages). *Picnic area to R. Château de Joux perched up on hilltop to R ahead, a 1000-year-old castle with an extensive series of dungeons and housing the Musée d'Armes Anciennes, a collection of rare weapons.*

KSO again. Reach junction with main road (L) to Neuchâtel in the hamlet of **Le Frambourg** *(note wayside Chapelle Saint-Léger to L at entrance)*. *Tabac/presse, bakery, bar/resto, pizzeria.*

KSO, go over railway line, pass hotel on L (*Auberge au Château de Joux 03.81.69.42.36), and 800m after that reach the

6km Junction with the D6 (752/193)

Bar/hotel/resto at junction, Hostellerie La Fontaine Ronde.

Turn L here (marked 'Les Fourgs 6, Sainte-Croix 15, Yverdon 34'), uphill. 1km later CH signed in Montpetot (1.5km off route, 03.81.69.42.50). Picnic tables in small lay-by on L, 2.5km from the start of the D6.

Turn L onto minor road to **Les Petits Fourgs** (two hamlets), veering R by way-side cross. Continue through both parts (ie 'Dessous' and 'Dessus' – 'lower' and 'upper'), veer R and then L to rejoin the D6 1.5km later (this was a short-cut). Turn L and shortly afterwards reach entrance to

6km Les Fourgs (758/187) Pop. 1058, 1100m

A very long, straggling village. TO (Grande Rue 36), superette, 3 restos (1 with bar/tabac), bakery. Gîte de France at 109 Grande Rue. Le Montagnon, Maison d'Hôtes, Grande Rue 20ter (03.81.69.44.03) on R near TO.

KSO along **Grande Rue** (out of village and KSO on D6 for 3.5km to the bor-der with **SWITZERLAND**. You are now in the Canton of the Vaud.
- *You will notice one or two changes almost immediately –*
- *benches positioned in scenic spots inviting you to sit down and rest*
- *yellow signs telling you how far it is (in time) to the next place on foot*
- *cows with cowbells*
- *a lot of fountains in public places (normally safe to drink)*
- *plenty of cafes/restos in small places.*

Remember that now you are in Switzerland you can no longer (normally) use euros.

The Via Francigena is waymarked in Switzerland as the TP (tourisme pédes-tre) route 70. The general yellow signage is very thorough, although at present the VF stickers themselves, used in parallel, are not yet as frequent, as a form of reas-surance, as the pilgrim (as opposed to the hiker) might like them to be.

3.5km Douane (761.5/183.5) 1108m

Border post. This is not manned, but Switzerland operates a system of *patrouilles volantes* (ie roving customs checks in cars). Bar/resto/hôtel La Grande Borne on Swiss side (024.454.30.30).

Continue ahead on road for 2km to

2km L'Auberson (763.5/181.5) 1110m

2 shops, fountain (with *eau potable*), café, bakery/tea shop. La Grange,

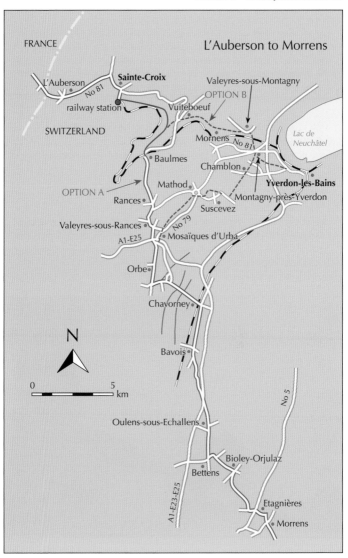

L'Auberson to Morrens

FRANCE

L'Auberson

No 81

Sainte-Croix

railway station

SWITZERLAND

Vuiteboeuf

Valeyres-sous-Montagny

OPTION B

Mornens

No 81

Lac de Neuchâtel

Baulmes

Chamblon

OPTION A

Mathod

Yverdon-les-Bains

Rances

Montagny-près-Yverdon

Suscevez

Valeyres-sous-Rances

No 79

A1-E25

Mosaïques d'Urba

Orbe

Chavorney

N

0   5 km

Bavois

Oulens-sous-Echallens

Bioley-Orjulaz

A1-E23-E25

Bettens

No 5

Etagnières

Morrens

177

Grande Rue 45–47, has rooms (024.454.43.77). CH at Grande Rue 97. Maison de la Paroisse at 66. Bus service to Sainte-Croix (from border) and from there to Yverdon. Musée Baud (musical boxes). (Switzerland, as you will discover, has museums for all sorts of things – including organs, games, cameras, fashion, wine labels and science fiction.)

KSO on road through village and then KSO ahead, steadily uphill, to the **Col des Etroits** (1153m), just after a junction, after which you descend along the **Avenue de Neuchâtel**, bending to L along **Rue des Arts**, to the **Place du Pont** in

4km Sainte-Croix (767.5/177.5) Pop. 4200, 1070m

CFF (railway station, changes money 7 days/week), shops, banks, etc. YH is now closed. The Paroisse Protestante organises a rota for pilgrim accommodation, but it is essential to phone ahead: 024.454.31.09. Hôtel/café du Centre, Rue Neuve (024.454.21.65), Hôtel de France, 25 Rue Centrale 25 (024.454.38.21). TO. Musée Cima (another musical-box museum).

Auberson church

Cyclists should continue from here down to Vuiteboeuf on the road (10km, 4km longer than the walkers' footpath option).

Walkers have the option of a quiet, shorter, well-waymarked TP route, although they should exercise caution in bad weather.

From the **Place du Pont** KSO then turn R, veering L, down **Avenue de la Gare**, to the railway station. Continue past it then KSO ahead on **Chemin de Mouille**, passing to LH side of railway tracks (this is TP 'Vuiteboeuf, Gorges de Covatannaz'), which then becomes a grassy track, veering L away from the railway line. 100m later turn R, veering L between fields. At next junction turn R, then immediately L, downhill, and KSO ahead. Path gradually veers L towards woods, crosses stream and veers R on other side towards a minor road.

KSO(R) ahead here, but 100m later look out for a TP sign indicating a RH turn through a turnstile to cross a field. Exit at the other side by a hairpin bend in a small road (*view of Lac de Neuchâtel and Yverdon-les-Bains ahead on a clear day*). Go downhill on road and 200m later, just past a farm building on L, turn R and then immediately L down steep tarmac track. Then, by a junction with a seat, turn R onto a stony track downhill through woods. KSO, downhill all the time, on a wide FP, with the river below you to the R. Cross bridge over the **Gorges de Covetannaz** and KSO ahead. Pass fountain (775m).

At fork in path take LH fork (do **not** turn hard L to bigger track and seats). KSO at next crossing then, shortly afterwards, go down a flight of steps to join wide forest track coming from back L. KSO(R) ahead, downhill again.

When you see a flight of steps with a handrail turning R uphill ahead of you, fork **left** downhill on FP with handrail to LH side. (*Church in Vuiteboeuf visible shortly afterwards through gap in the trees ahead.*) Emerge between houses on main road to Sainte-Croix by bend and road bridge over the river **Arnon**. Turn R, veering L, to hotel in

6km Vuiteboeuf (773.5/171.5) 600m

Hôtel/café/resto des Ours (024.459.22.59, open 7 days/week), shop.

Read ahead for the section from here to Orbe before you decide whether you want to go straight there (via Baulmes, Option A) or go via Yverdon-les-Bains (Option B), the route taken by Sigeric, stage number 56, but which, if you look at a map, involves a detour round two sides of a triangle. If you decide to go to Yverdon, note that the waymarked VF route does not lead you all the way there but indicates a pedestrian route (from just past Montagny) to the railway station

View over to Lac de Neuchâtel (Lake Geneva) and Yverdon-les-Bains

there. You will therefore have to backtrack the following morning to resume your journey.

If you do not wish to visit Yverdon, it is suggested that you take Option A. Both routes are nearly all on tarmac/concrete lanes – A is shorter and more direct, but B does have some shady sections through woods. Both are waymarked with the yellow TP (tourisme pedestre) signs and lozenges, but only Option B includes the VF signage as well.

OPTION A – DIRECT TO ORBE

Before you reach the hotel turn R onto a minor road and KSO, with the woods to your R, to a junction at the beginning of

3.5km Baulmes (777/168)

Shops, etc, CFF. **L'Auberge (a hotel), Rue Hôtel de Ville (024.459.11.18) and Hôtel du Jura, Rue Famenan (024.459.11.27).

At junction at the beginning of the village you can either KSO to visit it (and then retrace your steps) or turn L (**Rue de la Gare**) to continue and turn L over railway line (ie at end).

Open countryside. KSO then turn R at junction and KSO to

4km Rances (781/164)

Hôtel/café/resto L'Ecusson vaudois (024.426.99.90, X Sun pm), shop.

KSO through village, veering L and out on **Route de Valeyres** to

1km Valeyres-sous-Rances (782/163) 600m

La Vieille Auberge (café/resto, X Sun).

KSO on road through village past lavoir (L). KSO. 1km later, at junction with main road, turn R and continue on concrete track to its RH side then grassy track.

Cross bridge over motorway. KSO ahead at traffic lights, again on concrete track to RH side of road (concrete road to L under main road in dip leads straight to campsite).

KSO then veer L at roundabout (Route de Valeyres – campsite to L) then on **Avenue de Thienne** and **Grande Rue** to **Place du Marché** in Orbe.

OPTION B – ORBE VIA YVERDON-LES-BAINS

On the main road, with your back to the route coming from Sainte-Croix with VF signage, and facing the church on the hill in front of you, turn L along the road and 100m later, by fountain, turn L, marked 'Vugelles'. KSO ahead at a crossing between fields, leading to an industrial building by the main road. Turn R then immediately L over railway line and KSO on grassy/gravel track leading into the woods.

Pass **Refuge des Crêts** (a shelter with covered picnic table and seating) and KSO, gently downhill. Watch out carefully for a LH fork up a small but clear FP uphill, take it, and 200m later, at the top, turn L to cross the railway line again and then continue L on other side, veering R at junction onto gravel/grassy track. 500m later leave the woods, continue on a concrete path to a T-junction and turn L here to a farm at

4km Mornens, 538m

Turn R past house onto another concrete lane and then KSO ahead at crossing on **Chemin de Mornens** through woods. 800m later reach junction with **Chemin**

du Bois de Lily (coming from back R) and KSO ahead again, downhill. Go under railway line, turn L at T-junction and KSO towards another refuge, cross the railway line, KSO(L) uphill on other side and enter village on **Rue du Stand**. KSO(R) ahead at junction, veering R and then L into **Grande Rue** (no pavement), downhill towards the railway station in

2.5km Valeyres-sous-Montagny, 440m

Café/resto to L.

Cross the railway line and KSO on other side on track into woods, steeply uphill. At top (seat!), at a place known as **Le Gibet** (where executions took place until 1475) cross **Route du Crêt** and continue L downhill on **Chemin du Temple**. Pass church (L), veering R, and reach junction by **Service du Feu** in

1.5km Montagny-près-Yverdon, 450m

Café/resto (to R).

KSO(L) ahead between high concrete walls on **Chemin des Haies** ('hedge street'), cross **Route de la Perrausaz** and KSO on other side, crossing bridge over main road 300m later. KSO, then 800m after that reach a fork. This is where the VF signage tells you to KSO but where, if you want to go into Yverdon, you fork L marked 'Gare 40min' (and then return here the following day).

Yverdon-les-Bains, Pop. 24,000, 433m

All facilities, accommodation in all price brackets including Gîte du Passant, 14 Rue Parc (a backpackers' hostel, 024.425.12.33). Camping des Iris (024.425.10.89). TO 2 Avenue de la Gare (024.422.32.61.01, info@yverdon-les-bain.ch).

A spa town since Roman times at the southern end of Lake Neuchâtel. Roman military base built in AD325 with enormous ramparts and 15 masonry towers on an area of more than 2 hectares. Château, now the Musée d'Yverdon et Région, was built by the same architect as Caernarfon Castle in Wales. Stone circle dating from 3000BC. Musée Suisse de la Mode, La Maison d'Ailleurs (the only science-fiction museum in Europe). Stage LVI (Antifern, 56) in Sigeric's itinerary.

If you don't want to go into Yverdon continue ahead here, then 100m later turn R onto a concrete residential street, veering L and then R. Just before a large greenhouse complex (to your R, ahead), turn hard L uphill up wide track into woods (marked 'Chamblon, Mosaïques, Orbe'), veering R, uphill. Emerge at the top on a concrete track between fields, turn L and then R onto a bigger road leading to junction by church and café/resto in

3.5km Chamblon, 520m
Café/resto (X Mon).

Turn R past town hall and bus stop and then fork/veer L on **Rue des Chandelènes** (view over Yverdon-les-Bains at end). Cross main road and continue on **Rue du Pérou** on other side. KSO(L) at first fork by cemetery and KSO(R) at second (seats over to R) and KSO(R) at next fork. 400m after that fork R onto sandy/stony track between woods.

700–800m later turn L downhill on small concrete road then turn hard R onto another one. At junction KSO ahead on grassy track between fields, gently downhill towards the main road ahead. 250m before you reach it turn L through fields and then R on **Route de Susceraz** to a junction in

5km Mathod
Hotel/café/resto Le Bras d'Or (024.459.10.49). Shop. (From here the VF route does a detour, up behind the Route d'Orbe to the R.)

Turn L onto **Route d'Orbe**, passing shop (on L), cross bridge over small river and turn R up **Route des Champs du Pont**, veering L uphill then R. KSO. KSO(R) at junction up towards woods and then veer L alongside them, ignoring RH turns.

Part-way along (keep an eye out for small deer) turn R, veering L, into woods. KSO. Reach forest road coming from back R, turn L along it and KSO(R)

183

at junction immediately afterwards. 500m later, near signpost with VF marked route coming from R, KSO ahead.

Shortly aftwards leave the woods and KSO ahead on track coming from back L. KSO, then 70–80m later turn L across fields to HT pylon, and just after it turn R onto a concrete lane. At end, when lane veers R to join road passing at right angles in front of you, turn L below it, continue until you are level with road, then KSO(L) ahead to go under the main road. On other side turn second R on concrete lane between fields. At end turn R alongside motorway below you and either turn L to cross the bridge and continue or turn R to visit the Roman mosaics (see below) in the metal building to your R.

Having crossed the bridge, cross a road and KSO ahead. Turn R up a small tarmac road at the end then turn next L on **Route du Signal**, passing to LH side of campsite. Pass tennis courts and continue ahead to a roundabout (large supermarket to R) and fork L onto **Avenue de Thienne** and KSO and follow **Grande-Rue** to **Place du Marché** in

---

6.5km (4km via Option A) Orbe (786/159) Pop. 5819, 480m

All facilities. TO Grand-Rue 1 (024.442.92.37). CFF. Hôtel du Chasseur, Rue Sainte-Claire 2 (024.441.67.80). Hôtel/Motel des Mosaïques on outskirts at entry (024.441.62.61). Camping du Signal, Route du Signal (024.441.38.57).

Small town situated in a bend in the river Orbe with medieval streets surrounding the market square. Two towers left from the original castle, one of which, the Tour Ronde, was built in 1233 and offers a splendid view over the whole region. Rue du Moulinet has the oldest stone bridge in Switzerland (a humpbacked one dating from 1424), the mill dam and the former ROD flour mill. Mosaïques romaines d'Orbe-Boscéaz, containing nine very well-preserved mosaics from the largest Roman villa to have been discovered north of the Alps. Open daily from Easter to the end of October. Musée d'Orbe (art and local history). Eglise de Montcherand, 2km away, worth a visit for its 12th-century frecoes. Stage LX (Urba, 55) in Sigeric's itinerary.

Both routes From **Place du Marché** go down **Rue Centrale** and continue on **Rue du Grand Pont**. Cross the river **Orbe** and turn L on other side (**Route de Saint-Eloi**), crossing railway line and veering L past large factory. KSO(L) ahead on **Route des Granges Saint-Martin** then turn R (**Route de Chavornay**, but not marked) on road that has railway line to RH side and cycle track to L, passing **Gare Industrielle**.

KSO, cross three canals and continue to

Orbe, castle and church

5km Chavornay (791/154) 450m
SCRB. Hôtel/resto de la Gare (024.441.41.13). Pharmacy, bakery.

When cycle track go into station, cross via underpass and come out on other side on **Rue de la Gare**. At roundabout turn R and KSO until you reach

3km Bavois (794/151)
Abri PC (shelter, via Rue du Collège).

Continue ahead, uphill. *(A path off to L under viaduct is a short-cut.)* Cross motorway and KSO to

5.5km Oulens-sous-Echallens (799.5/145.5)
Café/resto.

Fork L on entry on **Rue du Bourget** (fountain and lavoir at end), turn L then R to church (**Rue du Centre/Rue du Dime**), and then KSO(L) on **Route de Bettens** to

1.5km Bettens (801/144)
Café/resto (X Sun after 4.00pm and Mon).

Turn L just before petrol station the KSO(R) at fork 400m later. KSO, pass gravel works, and at junction just before entry to **Bioley-Orjulaz** turn R (marked 'Lausanne, Boussens'). 300m later, just after a more minor road joins from back R, cross the Bioley-Orjulaz to Boussens road by a wayside cross and KSO on clear gravel track on other side towards woods. Veer L at bend and then turn R (seat) onto tarmac path, and then KSO(R) at fork.

KSO, mainly shady, for 2km, following road round and ignoring turns. Leave woods, KSO, veer R at T-junction by large barn and continue on road to main road by the railway station in

5.5km Etagnières (806.5/138.5) 628m

Bakery/groceries, Hôtel-Auberge d'Etagnières (X Mon).

Cross road and go up **Rue des Crêtes**, following it round. When houses stop it becomes a tarmac track, then 150m later turn R onto wide concrete pathway with small canal to R. 200m later turn L, then turn R 100m later onto gravel track.

At T-junction with concrete track turn L, uphill, then veer R at top to a minor road and KSO(R) along it for 100m, then turn hard L uphill into woods. 300m later reach minor road at top and turn L (ridge with good views on a clear day, seats), veering R down into **Place du Village** in

2km Morrens (808.5/136.5)

Café, fountain.

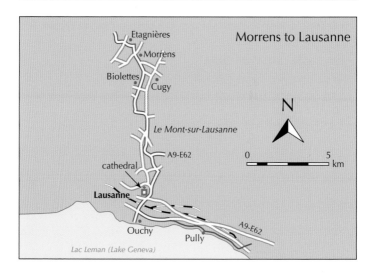

KSO(R) ahead on **Route du Cugy** then, just after bend to L by **Grande Salle** (plan of the commune on wall), turn R into **Rue des Biolettes** (*this is also a cycle track to Lausanne*). Road veers L and continues between fields. Cugy visible ahead. KSO.

When the **Route des Biolettes** turns R, do the same, entering **Les Biolettes** (a hamlet), at the end of which the road veers L downhill, crosses a small river and goes back uphill, veering R and then L into an industrial estate on the outskirts of

5.5km Le Mont-sur-Lausanne (814/131)

Continue ahead to the main road (**Route de Cugy**) and turn R along it (pavement), opposite the Budron bus stop. 300m later pass the Fougères bus stop (café opposite does food) and 50m after that turn L up gravel track (marked 'Exploitation forestière autorisée'), uphill into woods. At T-junction at the top turn R onto a slightly bigger track and KSO.

500m later reach T-junction with a small tarmac road (**Chemin des Fougères**) coming from L and KSO along it back to the **Route de Cugy**. Turn L, passing the Etavez bus stop and KSO (old milestone on L tells you it is 6km to Lausanne). KSO for 400m more to junction with small roundabout and Grand-Mont bus stop, continue ahead and 100m later turn L up **Chemin Creux**. At junction at end turn R onto **Route du Jorat**, leading down to another junction, **Place de Coppoz**, in

2km Coppoz (816/129) 702m

Hôtel Central (with bar/resto, 024.652.01.46), bakery, bank.

Lac Leman and Lausanne cathedral

KSO ahead on **Route de Coppoz** (tree-lined, seats, to L of Route de Lausanne), passing the **Temple du Mont-sur-Lausanne** (*a Protestant church – the original building dates from 1414, and the present one was built 1796–97*). KSO to **Place du Petit Mont**, a small five-point junction (with café/resto), and then continue ahead on **Route des Martines**, slightly downhill all the time.

KSO for 1km then cross motorway (*good views out over Lac Leman – Lake Geneva – ahead if no haze*) and enter the city of Lausanne. Turn first L at junction, slightly uphill, on **Route de la Clochatte**. KSO at junction 200m later then, 200m after that, fork R up **Chemin des Celtes**, entering the **Bois de Sauvabelin**, a very large wooded park, and continue to the **Lac du Sauvabelin** (663m, with two café/restos). *Here you meet the Via Jacobi (Chemin de Saint-Jacques) waymarks for pilgrims going to Santiago (signed with the yellow markers of TP4), which you then follow all the way to the cathedral and the centre of Lausanne.*

Continue ahead past both cafés, fork R at fork and then immediately L to reach the **Tour de Sauvabelin**, an enormous lighthouse-like tower, 35m high, with views over the whole area. *Visits possible, free of charge (9.00am–5.00pm, 6.00pm or 7.00pm according to season – worth a visit on a clear day – if you have a good head for heights!)*. Turn L shortly afterwards, then at a junction KSO(L) at fork ahead (not waymarked) and reach the **Chemin de la Chocolatière** by Le Signal bus stop, car park and a large wooden building that looks like a former market hall.

Old market hall, Signal du Mont

KSO(L) ahead here through park to viewpoint by chapel *(with spectacular views on a clear day with no haze, drinking fountain behind it)*, then backtrack a few metres to turn L onto small FP (before you reach a café), zigzagging downhill. Turn L at junction with another small path then, almost immediately, turn L onto a small FP then R onto a bigger TP downhill, leading to the **Fondation de l'Hermitage** (an art museum, with another café). Turn L in front of it onto a small FP, then turn L again onto a smaller path, through woods, downhill, stepped. KSO(L) ahead at fork and emerge by house No 18 on **Rue de la Barre** at the bottom. Turn L to junction (**Place du Nord**) with fountain.

KSO ahead (on **Rue de la Barre**), passing to L of Château Saint-Maire. Cross **Place du Château** and continue ahead on **Rue Cité Devant** to the cathedral, turning R to its entrance, in

---

3km Lausanne (819/126) Pop. 131,000

Altitude varies – Le Mont-sur-Lausanne, at the top of the town, is 900m above sea level, the centre 495m and the lakeside 370m. Large city with all facilities. CFF with trains to all parts of Switzerland and other European destinations. Regular ferry service from Lausanne along the coast of the lake to Vevey, Montreux and Villeneuve and back leaves from the port in Ouchy. 2 x TO, both open daily – Place de la Gare 9 (in main hall in station) and Place de la Navigation 4, by port (021.613.73.73, information@lausanne-tourisme.ch).

Accommodation in all price brackets, including YH (Jeunotel), Chemin du Bois de Vaix 36 (021.626.02.22, lausanne@youthhostel.ch). To go there follow Saint James waymarks through town and out via Vallée de la Jeunesse until they lead you to cross a major road by an underpass. Do not do this, but turn R instead along Avenue de Chavannes and then turn L into Chemin du Bois de Vaix. (At the time this guide was prepared a Lausanne city bus pass was included in the price.) Lausanne Guesthouse, Chemin des Epinettes 4 (021.601.80.00, info@lausanne-guesthouse.ch), a backpackers' hostel near rear of main railway station, K. Camping de Vidy, Route de Vidy, on edge of town to west, near lake.

If you want to buy maps while you are in Lausanne go to Payot, a large bookshop in Place Pepinet (off Rue Centrale) which has a good selection. But be warned – Swiss maps are very expensive! Internet at Quanta, Place de la Gare 4, and Espace Saint-François, Place Saint-François 12; otherwise ask in TO.

The present city is built on the side of the Mont-de-Lausanne, sloping down to the edge of Lac Leman (Lake Geneva), but the original town

Eglise Saint-François

(Losanna) was a Roman settlement near the lake dating back to15BC on a site occupied since the Mesolithic era. Gothic cathedral, 12th and 13th centuries, consecrated by Pope Gregory X in 1275, but in 1536, with the Reformation, it became a Protestant cathedral. It has 105 stained-glass windows, but of particular interest is its early 14th-century Portail Peint, an entrance on its south side which has recently been restored, with fine painted stone carvings in its tympanum and archway. Cathedral open daily 7.00am–7.00pm (closes earlier in winter), PS in 'Accueil' inside (ask there about possible pilgrim-only accommodation).

Other sights include the Château de Maire, built 1397–1426 to serve as a new Episcopal palace (today the seat of the cantonal government, but not open to the public). Eglise Saint-François, only surviving remains of an important Franciscan monastery built 1260–80 (the upper part and present-day windows date from 1370–87, and the belfry from about 1400). Eglise Notre-Dame-de-Valentin, the first Catholic church built after the Reformation. Tour de l'Ale, watchtower built in 1340 and one of the few surviving remains of the old city, Place du Palud, 17th-century hôtel de ville. Several museums. Stage LIV (Losanna, 54) in Sigeric's itinerary.

To continue from Lausanne you have two options as far as Villeneuve. See Section 6 for full details of each one.

OPTION A – BY FERRY

Do as did the pilgrims of old when they encountered uncrossable rivers, lakes and seas en route (and as you will have done to cross the English Channel) – take a boat! The boats leave from the *débarcadère* in Ouchy.

OPTION B – ON FOOT (1–2 DAYS)

Continue along the side of the lake via Vevey, Montreux and the Côtes de Lavaux (a very large vineyard area) to Villeneuve (37km). The route is built up for most of the way. The path is well waymarked with the normal yellow TP signs and lozenges and reasonably well with the VF (TP70) waymarking. It goes along the water's edge for a large part of the way, on everything ranging from small FPs along the beach to wide tarmac (but traffic-free) roads.

There is a certain amount of shade (and seats), but although later on you walk along the *quais* lined with flower beds, for the first part you have the lake to your R and the tall hedges of big private properties to your L, with the exception, near the start, of the Espace Général Guisan, a sculpture park open to the public from March to October (9.00am–7.00pm or 6.00pm, open the gate). Later the path takes you away from the lake and the waterfront through vines, up and downhill on very minor roads.

As there are a great many cafés, restaurants and (mainly expensive) hotels along the way, these have not been indicated for each place. The same applies to the bus services operating between Lausanne and Villefranche.

LAUSANNE TO THE GREAT ST BERNARD PASS

Approaching the col of the Great St Bernard Pass and the Combe des Morts

SECTION 6

Lausanne to the Great St Bernard Pass (126km)

To leave Lausanne, with your back to the main doors of the cathedral go down the **Escalier du Marché** opposite (crossing a busy road via an underpass part-way down) and reach **Place du Palud** at the bottom, with the hôtel de ville and a colourful painted statue of Justice in the centre. Turn L down **Rue du Pont**, cross **Rue Centrale**, then go up **Rue Saint-François** to the **Place Saint-François**. Pass to RH side of church, cross **Rue du Grand-Chêne**, go along **Rue du Petit-Chêne** steeply downhill, turn first L into **Rue Edouard Gibbon** *(named after the English historian Edward Gibbon, author of 'The History of the Decline and Fall of the Roman Empire')* and then R at end down **Rue de la Grotte**. Cross **Avenue de la Gare** and continue ahead on **Avenue d'Ouchy**. Go under the railway bridge, by Closelet bus stop, after which you have a choice.

OPTION A – BY FERRY TO VILLENEUVE

To take the ferry option continue ahead here on **Avenue d'Ouchy** and KSO down to the end, opposite the TO (where you can buy your ticket) and the port. The ferry runs three times a day (90 minutes including a change at Vevey).

OPTION B – ON FOOT (1–2 DAYS)

To continue along the lakeside turn L here, down **Avenue de Montchoisi**. KSO, pass junction with **Avenue de Jurigaz** (to L) and **Chemin de Montolivet** (to R), pass Montchoisi bus stop and 200m later, opposite a petrol station, turn R into a park onto a wooden FB. Turn R immediately (marked 'Sur les pas des renards') down a wooden ramp and then hard L onto a shady FP which veers R to continue through woods downhill alongside the river **Vuachère**. *This area is noted for its foxes.*

KSO but do **not** turn L over covered bridge over the river. Continue ahead instead on its RH side, downhill all the time, until you reach **Avenue de Denantou**, opposite houses No 10–18. Turn L, cross road bridge over the river then turn R into a park, on the **Chemin de la Vuachère**. Turn L immediately at fork (metal fox footprints embedded in the tarmac), veering R. Pass the Thai pavilion (on R), veering L to reach the **Quai d'Ouchy** by the **Tour Halidmund**. Cross the **Quai d'Ouchy**, turn L along the water's edge, cross a FB over a river and continue ahead on the **Sentier des Rives du Lac**, a FP. Enter the commune of

3.5km Pully (822.5/122.5)

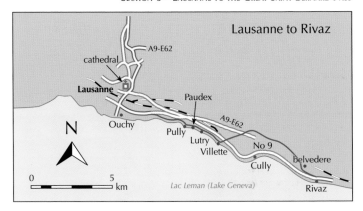

KSO. When the path stops, cross a carpark and veer R to the water's edge again (by the ferry stage) and then go round the yacht basin, veering L. Turn R by restaurant and continue on **Sentier du Lac Lutry**. Continue on **Chemin des Bains**, which becomes the **Chemin de la Plage**. Cross the **Paudèze** (a small river) and continue on **Chemin du Port**. You are now in the commune of Paudex.

KSO. Pass small building with a dome on top and KSO along the lakeside to the ferry landing stage in

2km Lutry (824.5/120.5) 373m
Now a part of the urban area around Lausanne, but originally a small medieval town, with its 11th-century Eglise Saint-Martin (worth a visit if you have time) and 16th-century castle.

From here to the Château de Chillon you will be walking below, and sometimes through, the Côtes de Lavaux, Switzerland's largest vineyard area. Its 830 hectares of terraced vines slope down to the lakeside, and as you walk through them you will find explanatory notices about the different crus (vintages) and their producers. The estates forming the area were cleared by Cistercian monks from Burgundy in the 12th century and planted with vines, an activity which has continued uninterrupted until the present day.

Turn L along side of yacht basin and then R back along the water's edge again, where the path becomes the **Quai Vaudaire**. When this ends the path continues along the beach (shingle) for a while, then on a small FP along the lakeside again.

195

Lakeside notice, from one dog to another…

Cross a small river and KSO. Cross a small concrete FB over small yacht basin and KSO. When FP comes to an end turn L up a flight of steps to road (**Route de Lavaux**) and turn R along it (extensive vineyards rising uphill on slopes to its LH side). The road becomes the **Route de Lausanne** and enter

2km Villette (826.5/118.5)

Continue ahead on road, and turn R opposite railway station (halt) to go under road and the railway line. Turn R on other side on **Chemin de Villette**. Continue through village, pass church (on R but entrance only from main road below). After that continue ahead, up and down, between vines on minor concrete road, the **Chemin de Courseboux**. At end go downhill, pass behind large parking area (to R) and reach railway station in

3km Cully (829.5/115.5) Pop. 1800, 370m
Shops, etc, hotels. TO by station.

Turn L, past TO (to R), and in front of café (L) turn R downhill to go under railway line on **Rue de la Gare** (shop at junction). Turn L on other side to church (ie a temple, as it is Protestant), pass to R of it on **Rue du Temple** then turn R by fountain (with another colourful statue of Justice in the middle) onto **Rue Davel**. KSO ahead at junction with **Place de l'Hôtel de Ville** and reach **Place d'Armes** by lakeside and ferry landing stage and turn L along the water's edge.

Continue to yacht basin and KSO on **Esplanade Docteur Charles Rochat**. Pass municipal campsite (Camping Moratel, 20/3–20/10), then veer L and then turn R by its office on minor (not main) road. Continue past yacht basin and restaurant (R) alongside the water's edge until you reach a flight of steps. Turn L and go under first the railway line (by Espesses railway halt) then under the road (or turn R and continue on the road to Rivaz, as the TP takes you high up above the road) and up (a lot!) more steps (this is the **Sentier du Vieux Moulin**) to **Le Crêt Dessous** (a hamlet). Turn hard R there onto the **Chemin de Calamin**, a concrete road through vineyards, well above the lake below – this is the touristic **Chemin des Vignerons**. KSO!

No shade at all, although in a couple of places the proprietors of the vineyards have provided a tonnelle with a covered picnic table and seats for passers-by (and pilgrims…) to rest. Every square inch of land in this area has been planted, and you can see the modern methods used today – the teleferic apparatus used for bringing down the grapes to the road during the vendages (harvest period), for example.

The path (ie the concrete road) becomes the **Chemin de Dezaley** (the name of the classification of all the wines in the area). KSO and 3km later reach a junction of similar roads with a small wayside chapel and a *belvédère* (viewpoint) with trees and seats. After this the road descends steeply on the **Chemin de la Dame**. Turn R over river on **Chemin de Forestay** to junction with covered fountain in

4.5km Rivaz (834/111) 400m

Café/restos.

Turn L up **Rue du Collège**, and then L again up **En Bons Voisins** (a street), then R along **Chemin de Rosset** (house on L has rooms), passing cemetery, along side of hill. This becomes **Chemin des Paleyres**, leading gradually downhill through vines again, passing beneath the ruins of a castle high above you to L. KSO ahead at junction (on **Chemin de la Vigne à Gilles**).

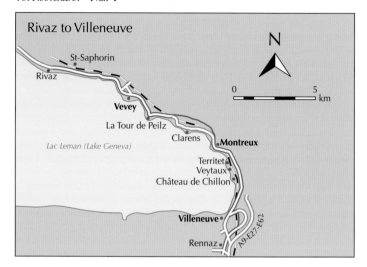

Rivaz to Villeneuve

N

St-Saphorin

Rivaz

0   5 km

Vevey

La Tour de Peilz

Clarens   **Montreux**

Lac Leman (Lake Geneva)

Territet
Veytaux
Château de Chillon

Villeneuve

Rennaz   A9·E27·E62

When you cross a river shortly afterwards look up (L) to a chalet above you where a very realistic-looking dummy, in bleu de travail (work clothes) sits at a table at the window on the first floor, obviously enjoying a bottle...

Continue ahead to another junction (tree and seat) and then go steeply downhill on **Chemin du Mont** to the church in

1.5km Saint-Saphorin (835.5/109.5) 405m

The **waymarked path** (no shade) leads you ahead here under an arch and then turns L, veering R, uphill again along the hillside on the **Sentier des Rondes**. This brings you out, 3km later, passing under the railway line at the entrance to Vevey.

Alternatively – KSO(R) ahead, marked for the railway station, then turn L alongside church along **Chemin Neuf** (*note old wine press, under cover, shortly afterwards on L*). Reach road and KSO along it (pavement), parallel to lake – the amount of traffic varies, but no shade at all.

Pass sign to campsite (La Pichette) some 1.5km later, leading R over a bridge over the railway line. Turn R onto it, then turn L onto a minor road which returns you to the **Route de Lausanne** 1km later in **Corseaux**, when the latter crosses the railway line, 1km before you reach Vevey. KSO.

Pass notice board with large street plan by town entrance board, pass the **Nestlé head offices** (on R) and continue to a roundabout (the VF waymarked route joins here from back L) and fork R on **Avenue Nestlé**, marked 'Vieille Ville'. KSO, cross the river **Veveyse**, after which the road becomes **Rue du Torrent**, and 900m later reach the **Place du Marché/Grande Place** by the waterfront in the centre of

4km Vevey (839/106) Pop. 18,000, 383m

Busy resort town with all facilities and accommodation in all price brackets, mainly 'high end', but including Riviera Lodge, a backpackers' hostel (+ K), Place du Marché 5 (021.923.80.40, www.rivieralodge.ch). Pension Famille Bürgle, Rue Louis-Meyer, 16 (021.921.40.32). TO in La Grenette, a former grain market hall in Place du Marché/GrandePlace 9 (084.886.84.84).

Vevey's sights include the Eglise Saint-Martin, 15th century (up the hill), and several museums including the Musée Suisse de l'Appareil Photograhique (cameras), Musée Suisse du Jeu (games), Alimentarium (food) and the Musée Historique de Vevey (free admission). (A museum devoted to the life and work of Charlie Chaplain, a resident in Vevey for many years, is in preparation.) Many other famous people – including writers, artists and musicians – spent considerable time in Vevey, including Ernest Hemingway, Dostoievsky, Kokoschka, Graham Greene, Jean-Jacques Rousseau, Victor Hugo, Gandhi, Le Corbusier, Gustave Eiffel and Freddie Mercury. Stage LIII (Vivaec, 53) in Sigeric's itinerary.

From Vevey to Villeneuve the lakeshore is almost continuously built up, but apart from a stretch in Clarens, where there are some very large properties whose gardens go down to the shore line, you can walk all the way to Villeneuve along the side of the lake, decorated with flower beds and offering a lot of shade in hot weather.

To continue, cross the **Place du Marché/Grande Place** and turn L along the lakeside on **Quai Perdonnet**. Continue on **Quai Roussy** and enter the commune of **La Tour-de-Peilz** (note floral sculptures in park to L). At end, **Place du Four**, with **Musée Suisse du Jeu**, KSO again on FP, veering L then R through stone doorway to continue ahead past yacht basin.

KSO on FP, and after crossing FB turn L up steps and emerge on **Route de Saint-Maurice** opposite La Becque bus stop. Turn R along it for 1km (pavement), then by Burier bus stop leave the road briefly, forking R downhill on FP, passing La Maladaire campsite (with café/resto). Go up slope at end and enter the commune of **Clarens**.

KSO on road, which then becomes **Rue du Lac**. 700m later, by yacht basin, return to water's edge on **Quai de Clarens**. KSO on **Quai J-J Rousseau**, **Quai de Vernex** and **Quai Ed. Jaccoud** to the ferry landing stage in

10km Montreux (849/96) 375m

TO by port (Place de l'Eurovision). Accommodation mainly high end, but also includes Pension Wilhelm, Rue du Marché 13 (021.963.14.31). Nowadays a big resort town, Montreux developed in the 19th century to supply the growing demand for accommodation in an area much sought after, in particular by the English aristocracy.

Continue ahead on **Quai de la Rouvenaz**, passing **Montreux Casino** and the Quai des Fleurs (it lives up to its name) until you reach the landing stage in

2km Territet (851/94)

To sleep in the Montreux YH, Passage des Auberges 8 (021.963.49.34, montreux@youthhostel.ch) continue past the tennis club and turn L on road under the railway line (YH is first building on L).

Otherwise – KSO on **Quai Ami Chessex** and 2km later reach the

2km Château de Chillon (853/92) 373m

A 'fairy tale'-style castle-fortress built, 12th century onwards, on a rock on the lakeshore, to control the passage between the north and the south of Europe and used, at different times, as an arsenal, a prison and a princely residence. One of the most visited tourist attractions in Switzerland – open all year (X 25/12 and 1/1).

Continue ahead along the lakeshore. Path becomes **Quai des Correspondences**. When you pass the swimming pool (R), and before the road bridge over the railway line at the entrance to Villeneuve, turn R to continue along the water's edge, veering R to cross the river **Tinière** and then L back again to continue on **Quai des Correspondences** until you reach the ferry landing stage in

Château de Chillon

3km Villeneuve (856/89) Pop. 4100, 370m

SCRB. **Hôtel du Soleil, Grande Rue 20 (021.960.21.22), Restaurant Le Romantica (also a hotel), Grande Rue 34 (021.960.15.40), Hôtel/Restaurant de l'Aigle, Grande Rue 48 (021.960.10.04). Campsite.

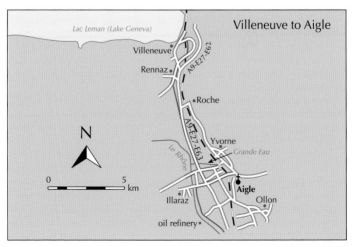

Lakeside town dating from Celtic times. TO in Place de la Gare by railway station, Mon–Fri only, in former Gothic chapel, the only surviving remains (with its 14th-century tower) of the former hospital. Eglise Saint-Paul, 12th-century origins.

The section from here to Aigle and Saint-Maurice is flat, although you have the mountains to either side, and it has a lot of industrial estates, arable land and hardly any shade. The route described here, on an almost traffic-free minor road to start with and then along the river as far as Saint-Maurice, does not coincide all the time with the VF waymarked one (which goes under the railway line at the side of the station in Villeneuve and then goes via Roche and Yvorne to Aigle and then via Ollon to Massongex), but it is direct, quiet, apart from the inevitable hum of the motorway in the distance, and mainly free of traffic. Note, however, that there are no cafés, no fountains or other services until you reach Aigle, and there is nowhere to sit down.

From the ferry landing stage go up **Rue du Collège** to **Place de la Gare** and then turn R into **Grande Rue**, then turn L at church into **Rue du Temple**, passing to L of it on **Rue de Poterlaz**. Go under **Rue des Remparts** then turn R into **Rue du Pont Noir**, a road used mainly by cyclists alongside the railway line and which you will follow half way to Aigle.

KSO, passing campsite (Les Bouleaux) on R. KSO, go under motorway, after which road veers R alongside it and then veers L to skirt its exit/junction. Continue to some traffic lights, then turn R to continue on cycle track to RH side of main road. Reach a roundabout and continue ahead on it (**Chemin de la Rotta**). When main road crosses railway line, cycle track doesn't follow it but continues to RH side of railway line. KSO.

When you get to **Roche** (4km) station you can turn L under the line (VF way-marked route comes through from here) and go up **Rue de la Gare** to visit the place (Hôtel Siol, Chemin de la Buanderie 2, 021.960.26.26), two cafés, Musée de l'Orgue) or for the campsite, then retrace your steps.

Otherwise, KSO along the railway line all the time. Pass turning (R) to **Yversey** (but to go to campsite cross bridge over line further on, as it is on the other side of the tracks). *Yversey was Stage LII (Burbulei, 52) in Sigeric's itinerary.* Pass turning under railway line to **Yvorne** (campsite), then KSO and cross **La Grande Eau** (a river) and go under flyover. Entering **Aigle** continue on **Chemin des Lieugex** until you reach a mini-roundabout. To go to the centre of the town turn L here up **Rue**

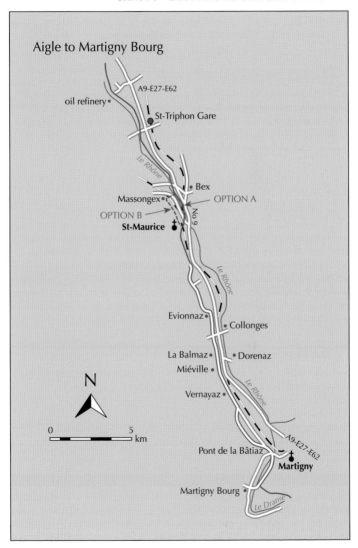

Aigle to Martigny Bourg

oil refinery

A9-E27-E62

St-Triphon Gare

Le Rhône

Bex

Massongex

OPTION A

OPTION B

No 9

St-Maurice

Le Rhône

Evionnaz

Collonges

La Balmaz

Dorenaz

Miéville

Vernayaz

Le Rhône

N

0   5
km

A9-E27-E62

Pont de la Bâtiaz

Martigny

Martigny Bourg

Le Dranse

de Rhône, go under railway lines, turn L **up Rue de la Gare** to **Place du Centre** and continue ahead on **Rue Colomb** to **Place du Marché** in

10km Aigle (866/79) Pop. 8000, 400m

Small town near the river Rhône with CFF, shops, banks, etc. TO Rue de Colomb. Hôtel Le Suisse, Rue de la Gare 28 (024.466.22.07), Auberge des Messageries, Rue du Midi 19 (024.466.20.60). Camping Les Glariers (024.466.26.60). The Château d'Aigle was built in 12th century but is now a wine, vineyard and wine-labels museum.

To continue, retrace your steps to the mini-roundabout (if you went into the town) and then continue ahead on **Route d'Evian** (or turn R along it if you didn't go into the centre of Aigle). Pass under the main Lausanne–Martigny road, cross the motorway and a small canal, go over a junction with another mini-roundabout then, 2km from Aigle, turn L along the LH bank of the river **Rhône** (a cycle track) just before you reach the Illaraz footbridge (389m). KSO.

There is some shade on this route, according to the time of day, but nowhere to sit down. Pass the **Pont de Saint-Tryphon** 5–6km later, and 2km after that pass the **Passarelle de Monthey** (396m), a wooden footbridge over the river. 2km later go under a road bridge and then, 600m later, reach the bridge at

13km Massongex (879/66)

You are now in the canton of the Valais. 2 café/restos by church (on the RH side of the Rhône). Campsite on LH side by bridge.

To continue you have a choice – both options are waymarked as walking routes but only Option B has the VF stickers.

OPTION A

KSO on the LH bank of the river, doing a 'kink' to L and then R to go over a river that empties into the **Rhône**, after which you KSO ahead again. 500m later tarmac stops, and route continues as a gravel track. Go under railway bridge and KSO. Track then goes uphill to lay-by with abstract sculptures, opposite a very large concrete wayside cross.

Cross road carefully, turn R downhill and then R again under road to château. Turn L (pavement) and KSO on **Route de Chablais** at the entrance to Saint-Maurice.

OPTION B

Turn R over the bridge and then L on the other side onto a cycle track along the RH bank of the **Rhône**. 1km later turn R to **Route de Chablais**, cross it, turn L, cross the railway line and turn L onto another cycle track on the other side (**Chemin de Saint-Maurice**). 800m later turn L under the railway line onto the **Route de Chablais** and turn R along it. Enter the town, passing below the castle (above you to R).

Both options Fork R at junction on **Rue d'Agaune** to the abbey in

3km Saint-Maurice (882/63) Pop. 3800, 419m

SCRB, CFF. TO Avenue des Terreaux 1 (024.485.40.40, info@saint-maurice. ch). The abbey has accommodation for a limited number of pilgrims (ask in office, PS). Space permitting, pilgrims can also be accommodated in the Foyer Franciscan (Avenue de Quartéry). Hôtel de la Dent du Midi, Avenue du Simplon 1 (024.485.12.09).

A first church on this site was already in existence in the fourth century, built by Theodule, bishop of Octodurus (the Roman name for Martigny), in honour of Saint-Maurice and his companions. Saint-Maurice was a Roman commander in the Theban army, put to death about AD300, along with numerous others, for refusing to kill the Christian soldiers fighting on the other side. What has become the Abbaye de Saint-Maurice d'Agaune was enlarged in AD515 by Saint-Sigismond, King of the Burgundians. It has been in existence, uninterrupted, since that time, so in 2015 it will be celebrating its 1500 years. The church has modern stained-glass windows by Edmond Bille depicting the life and work of Saint-Maurice.

Detail of entrance doors, Abbaye de Saint-Maurice

The abbey also has a splendid treasury which is well worth a visit, containing, amongst other things, the relics of Saint-Maurice himself and

Saint-Sigismond; guided tours daily (in several languages) which also include archeological excavations revealing the five different abbey churches that have been on the site. Mass 3 times daily on Sundays; lauds, vespers, etc, daily, which pilgrims are welcome to attend.

Saint-Maurice's other sights include the castle and its military history museum; the Grotte des Fées in the hillside near the town with its undergound lake and 77m waterfall; historical fortress with the subterranean Fort du Scex (1911–95); and Fort de Cindey (1941–95). Chapelle de Notre-Dame du Scex, perched up on the cliffs 120m above the town, mainly 18th century, and accessible by a flight of 500 steps. Eglise Saint-Sigismond, Chapelle Saint-Jacques (now closed). Stage LI (Sce Maurici, 51) in Sigeric's itinerary.

To continue, after visiting the abbey turn L opposite its church into **Place du Parvis** and then R into **Grande Rue** (TO at corner), lined with patrician houses, and turn R at end up to the railway station. Turn L in front of it, passing PO (on L). At end turn R over railway line on **Route des Cases** and then second L along **Avenue de Vérollier**, signposted for the chapel of that name. Cross river, KSO, and 400m later turn L to the

Hôpital Saint-Jacques, Saint-Maurice

1.5km Chapelle des Martyrs/Chapelle de Vérollier (883.5/61.5)

There has been a chapel on this site since before AD1000. Site of martyrdom of Saint-Maurice. Mass on 22nd of every month at 5.45pm (the date of his martyrdom), unless it falls on a Sunday (when mass will be said on 21st). Open 1/5–31/1, but no Sunday mass. Restored 1982.

After visiting, pass to LH side of **Maison de la Famille** (the big building next door) on small FP then turn R behind it, veering L across grassed area to LH corner with another small FP alongside hedge on L, veering L alongside a field. *(This section also coincides with the Itinéraire des Chapelles, a local walking route)*. Turn R along an embankment then L to the side of a stone wall leading to a road. Turn R and then immediately L by very tall wayside cross (marked 'Les Emonets'), climbing gradually. Passing behind café/resto in hamlet of **Les Emonets** (440m).

KSO ahead, uphill all the time, passing lavoir (R) with fountain, just before a junction, after which the route continues on the **Chemin de l'Acquis**, a shady walled lane for a while. At T-junction 300m later at end, turn L then immediately R on shady gravel track, along line of HT pylons above. KSO.

Cross river by sturdy wooden FB, after which path descends a little. Reach T-junction with minor road 1km later and turn L on it, downhill, veering L to junction at **Les Presses** (487m), with another covered lavoir and fountain. KSO(R) ahead on **Chemin de la Presse** (coming from back L) and 800m later cross the **Ancienne Route Cantonale** (a main road). Continue ahead on **Chemin Vieux** on other side to **Place de la Fontaine** and church in the centre of

5.5km Evionnaz (889/56) 469m

PO, shop, 2 cafés (1 with resto).

KSO on **Rue Principale** and rejoin **Ancienne Route Cantonale** at end (coming from back R). Cross over and fork R down **Chemin du Stade** passing behind large sawmill. *A lot of this section, as far as Vernayaz, is shady and more or less flat.* Partway along route it becomes **Chemin d'Amont**. KSO and join road by large wayside cross in

3km La Balmaz (892/53) 449m

Café/resto.

KSO on **Rue des Echelles** (not marked at start) and continue to end to main road (**Route de la Cascade**). KSO for 500m, passing petrol station with café/resto and KSO. 200m later fork R on **Rue de Miéville** into hamlet of

1km Miéville (893/52)

Lavoir/fountain with picnic table, all under cover.

KSO, then 100m later fork R off road, marked 'Salanfé', and pass behind a hotel/café/resto and continue parallel to, but not next to, a canal, veering R to a spectacular waterfall, the **Cascade de Pissevache**. Turn L on FP through trees, parallel to cliffs above R, mainly shady and parallel to the main road (audible but not visible) over to L. KSO.

When track ends, by Vernayaz shooting range, turn L then R along canal bank (LH side) and continue to junction on **Chemin de Rantze**. Turn L by very large electricity substation, veering R, past large wayside cross, pass behind **Boulodrome William** on **Chemin vers Le Mont**. KSO. Pass cemetery (L) and KSO on **Chemin des Condémines** to main road in

2km Vernayaz (895/50) 455m

Turn R, pass entrance to **Gorges de Trient** (on R, ticket office does coffee and cold drinks) to the Hotel/café/resto Le Pont de Trient and cross railway line. After bend, fork R down grassy slope onto FP by hut, continuing on wide shady footpath through woods. After waterworks building on R (with fountain) turn R over two FBs and KSO ahead. At T-junction turn R and KSO, following path round through woods. At next junction, with field to L, KSO.

1km later, with orchards to L, the path goes slightly uphill, crosses a depression with enormous boulders in it, and then continue ahead with orchards to your L, then woods to both sides.

Pass behind another large electricity substation, go up slope and continue on FP to L of crash barrier on main road into Martigny (coming from back R), joining it

Covered bridge at La Bâtiaz, entrance to Martigny

at entrance to town. KSO. KSO to RH side of road at junction by garage then fork R, marked 'La Bâtiaz'. Pass junction of many TP paths and sitting area (on L), and KSO to cross the river **Dranse** by the **Pont de Bâtiaz**, a covered wooden bridge. Turn R on other side (castle high above you to R) and then turn (not fork) L into **Rue de la Dranse**. Turn first R, veering L, on **Rue de la Fusion** (not marked at start), cross road, go up steps into **Place du Manoir** (a large open space), cross it diagonally, pass five large tubular structures and then continue L ahead along the side of a large super-market on **Rue des Ecoles** to **Place Centrale** and the hôtel de ville in

5km Martigny (900/45) Pop. 15,050, 471m

Medium-sized town with all facilities. CFF. Accommodation in all price brackets, including Camping TCS (Route de Levant, 027.722.45.44), which also has a dormitory. Pilgrims can also enquire about simple accommodation at the Paroisse Catholique, Rue de l'Hôtel de Ville (in centre, 027.72.22.82). TO Avenue de la Gare 6 (027.720.49.49, info@martignytourism.ch).

Note If reserving hotel accommodation make sure you check whether it is in the town itself or in Martigny Bourg (3km further on, uphill) or Martigny Croix (4km).

Commercial centre since Roman times, with significant Gallo-Roman remains. The town's main sights include the Château de la Bâtiaz, the Fondation Pierre Giannada (an art museum) and Le Musée et Chiens du Saint-Bernard. Hôtel de ville houses the largest stained-glass window in Switzerland, completed in 1948, recounting the history of the town.

Church door at Martigny

KSO ahead on other side of square along side of 'Accueil Citoyen' (on L), cross **Rue du Simplon**, passing church (on R), and continue on to **Rue de l'Octodure**, then turn R almost immediately (opposite house No 5) and then L in front of a block of flats to go along side of parking area. Then turn R onto FP alongside an orchard, with hedge to L. Continue on FP, veering L past fountain and children's play area by Gallo-Roman remains then turn L into **Rue de l'Ouche**. At end turn R into **Rue du Forum**. Turn L along side of another parking area, go under railway line and then turn R (turn L here for campsite) onto **Rue du Levant**.

KSO, go under railway line, pass to RH side of Martigny Bourg railway station, then, when road veers R, KSO(L) ahead on **Rue du Chemin de Fer** past another parking area (L), veering R then L opposite fountain to **Place du Bourg** in

---

3km Martigny Bourg (903/42) 490m

SCR. Hôtel des Trois Couronnes, now a restaurant, dates from 1609. Le Moulin Semblanet, one of the oldest industrial-type mills in Switzerland, restored in 1994 and now classified as a historic monument.

Continue (L) up **Rue du Bourg** to the Place Saint-Michel at the top, with bell-tower and Chapelle de Saint-Michel. *There has been a chapel on this site since 1345, but the present building dates from 1649. Executions took place here in the square opposite the chapel, the last one in 1840.*

Continue ahead, past a roundabout with a sculpture in the middle, on **Avenue du Grand-Saint-Bernard**, passing below Martigny Croix railway station (L above), and before the bridge over the river **Dranse** turn L into a parking lot (fountain and picnic tables) and then read the next paragraphs (as far as Sembrancher) before you go any further.

*The valley up from Martigny Croix through Bovernier and up to Sembrancher is **very** narrow, with steep-sided cliffs on either side of the river Dranse, the road and the railway line in the valley bottom and, apart from the route described below, on narrow footpaths, there is no other option, either for bad weather, poor visibility, for those unused to this type of walking or for those who aren't very agile. You do not actually need a very good head for heights (this author has an extremely bad one), but you do need to be very careful if it is wet or windy, all the more so if you are alone. Do not, however, under any circumstances, consider walking on the road – this is only two lanes wide, is full of very fast-moving, heavy traffic, and there is rarely any hard shoulder or pavement to protect you. This is the worst section of the whole Via Francigena, all the way from Canterbury to Rome, and if you feel unable to tackle it for whatever reason you will have*

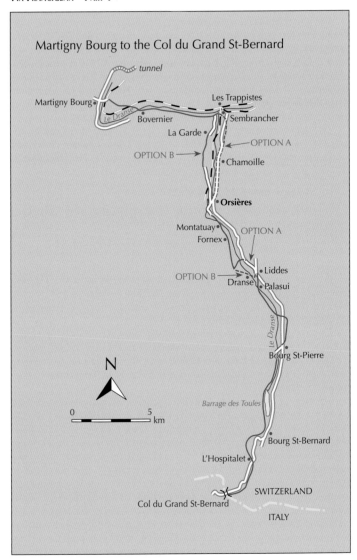

Martigny Bourg to the Col du Grand St-Bernard

to resign yourself, reluctantly, to taking the train (frequent service) for the 10km stretch from Martigny Croix to Sembrancher (after which you will not have any more problems).

If you are happy to continue (the waymarking is adequate if you are attentive), cross the parking area diagonally L and go up steps labelled 'Zurich parcoursvita' (a health circuit) to railway line, turn L, cross line 20m later and fork L uphill on wide track into woods, climbing gently, along the side of the railway line all the time (seats at intervals). 1km later cross back to RH side of track and KSO ahead, slightly downhill to start with.

KSO, pass wooden FB and gym frame (to L) and continue along side of river (on your R), then fork L uphill on narrower path with handrail. Go up flight of steps, under railway again, continue on small FP then turn L in small clearing, uphill. Turn R up more steps, then R again at top, on clear FP, undulating, veering L along side of hill. Clear path but be very careful in wet weather.

1km later fork L uphill on similar path. Cross FB, turn R then L downhill, then uphill, and at fork KSO(R) ahead, slightly uphill all the time. Reach a section with a chain handrail then one with a FB, turn R then L downhill, negotiate difficult steps (with chains) and continue along side of hill for a while. Another section with chains (path) follows, then cross a lot of very large boulders. KSO then reach junction (with signpost) and KSO(R) ahead downhill. Reach an open area planted with new vines and lines of metal supports and KSO ahead with these to L and river below to R.

200m later you have a choice. Either turn hard R to cross the river and then turn L on other side onto a tarmac lane, continue on wide wall and then go through vines and turn R onto road coming from next bridge over the river (to your L). Alternatively, continue on LH side of river and then turn R to cross second bridge.

Then (both options) continue, slighty uphill, to go under the railway and the road (fountain by cemetery gates) turn L and reach small square in the centre of

5km Bovernier (908/37) 620m
2 cafés, bank and PO to R, church ahead.

Turn L to continue. Reach main road, continue along it for 200m to a wood-yard, then fork R past it, and then fork R again to (very) large covered lavoir.

This route continues up and down through the woods all the time, on small FPs for the most part, although there are some sections where you just have to walk from one yellow waymarking 'lozenge' to the next, following them over rocks and boulders, with the **Dranse**, the road and the railway line down below you. Continue on this 'route' for 3.5km then, 1.5km before Sembrancher, come out of the woods, cross a stream and reach a junction with a wide gravel track at a bend. This is

3.5km Les Trappistes (911.5/33.5) 697m

KSO(R) ahead on wide track and continue alongside railway line for a while, then veer R uphill. KSO. 1km later reach a small tarmac road, turn L on bridge over railway and then R on other side. Then either enter station (L, café/resto, TO) and then continue ahead on **Avenue de la Gare**, or KSO ahead on **Route de la Gravanne** (not marked at start) which then meets **Avenue de la Gare** shortly afterwards. Continue on it, passing covered fountain (R) and church (near on R) and reach **Rue Principale** (shops) in the centre of

1.5km Sembrancher (913/32) Pop. 800, 717m

Large supermarket on L at entry. Hôtel de la Gare, with café/resto (027.785.11.14, hotelgaresembrancher-sg@hotmail.com). Camping de la Prairie (027.785.21.30).

Older-style wooden houses near station (which also houses TO), many of them *raccards* (storage barns for corn and other cereals). Eglise Saint-Etienne (1680), 16th-century Hospital de Sembrancher (now restored and serving as courthouse) provided board and lodging to pilgrims and itinerant workers.

Cross over in **La Place** (a street), veering R, then turn R (still La Place) and continue up **Rue Principale** through old part of the town and reach a junction where this turns L. Here you have a choice of routes to Orsières (a lower- and a higher-level route). Both routes are waymarked, but nothing at this stage indicates which one will be signed as the Via Francigena.

OPTION A – LOWER-LEVEL ROUTE

This passes to the LH side of the main road, is not a high as Option B and is on very quiet minor roads.

Turn L into the second part of **Rue Principale**, a street lined with old raccards, and reach the main road by a large wayside cross. Cross over and continue on a minor road (marked 'Chamoille') on **Route des Moulins**, cross a river and then turn R on other side (**Les Moulins**, 729m), zigzagging uphill, and at a junction (with seat) marked 'Combaillon' fork to L (marked 'Orsières'). KSO uphill to **Chamoille** (chapel open). Turn L for 'kink' in road (although there is a short-cut for the hairpin straight ahead marked 'bordiers autorisés'), then reach second part of Chamoille (920m) with wooden houses.

After this go downhill, and as you go round the corner Orsières becomes visible ahead. KSO, downhill all the time, passing white sign for the Commune of Orsières (and after which you see a sign indicating a fork uphill to the L to Orsières).

Do not take it, but KSO ahead, downhill all the time, and at the bottom cross the bridge over main road and continue L on other side. Join main road, and 600m after petrol station fork R, veering R into **Route de Saint-Bernard** at entry to village. KSO to junction by bridge, then either turn L (still Route de Saint-Bernard) to church, square, shops and hotels or, to continue, fork R up **Route de la Gare** to the railway and bus station in Orsières (see below).

OPTION B – HIGHER-LEVEL ROUTE

This is the Chemin Napoléon, a higher-level path than Option A, but mainly on grassy tracks. It is also, as you will discover, the one marked as the VF route.

KSO ahead at junction up **Route de Cleusuit**. Veer L and then turn R under railway, reach hairpin bend in road and KSO ahead up steep but clear and distinct FP. 200m after that reach a crossing with a similar FP, and KSO ahead up narrower FP to a junction with TP signs, VF stickers (and seat) and fork L uphill.

KSO (marked 'La Garde' at signpost) and continue uphill to emerge on open area with meadows to either side. KSO(L) ahead on clear gravel track coming from R. KSO. Reach road at bend and fork R uphill. At crossing KSO ahead on **Rue du Four** to **Place du Village** in the hamlet of

2km La Garde (915/30) 900m
Chapelle Saint-Grat (17th century).

KSO ahead (in front of chapel), pass fountain and turn R, forking L immediately on **Route des Grangettes**, downhill. *(Chamoille, on the other route, is visible to L on the other side of the valley.)* KSO, gradually downhill between meadows,

215

then turn L to cross FB over a stream (**La Ravenna**, 860m). Enter woods then fork L steeply downhill, marked for VF but also as 'Route Napoléon', and join a wider, flatter route coming from back L. KSO then return to woods.

Pass wayside cross and seat (above you to R) then an isolated house (1552) and KSO. At junction shortly afterwards (**Point**, 856m), KSO (marked 'Orsières 1h'). 1km later reach wide track, turn L and then, at bend, KSO(R) ahead on grassy/gravel track (view of Orsières ahead).

KSO, gently downhill. Go over level crossing and 1km after that reach main road at entrance to the town, opposite a petrol station. Turn R on **Route du Grand-Saint-Bernard** to the junction with **Route de la Gare**, then either turn L (still Route du Grand-Saint-Bernard) to church, square, shops and hotels or, to continue, fork R up **Route de la Gare** to the railway and bus station in

4km Orsières (919/26) Pop. 2600, 901m

Shop, Hôtel de l'Union, Rue de la Commune (027.783.11.38, info@chezjo. ch), Hôtel Terminus, Route de la Gare (027.783.20.40, info@grosminus.ch). TO in railway station, from where there is a bus service up to the Col du Grand Saint-Bernard (15/5–15/10) and trains down to Martigny and beyond. Parish accommodation available.

Eglise Saint-Nicholas, 11th–13th centuries, has very nice (modern representational) stained glass. Stage L (Ursiores, 50) in Sigeric's itinerary.

Orsières

Both routes now follow in the same direction. Pass to LH side of station building, turn L and then, with your back to the tracks, go down steps to R to cross the river **Dranse**. Turn R uphill on the **Route de Podemainge** (marked 'Montatuay, 40m, Dranse 2h, Liddes, 2h 15') then 400m later, at junction with road bridge over to R, KSO(L) ahead on smaller tarmac track. Cross bridge over river and veer R uphill on wide gravel track. KSO on this, zigzagging steeply uphill (mainly shady), ignoring junctions with small FPs, to **Montatuay**, 1060m, a collection of isolated houses. Continue ahead, then route joins from back R and goes downhill again for a while then levels out briefly. At fork KSO(R) ahead on the level, then at **Fornex** (fountain), 1216m, fork R after last house up grassy track (seat) veering R to woods.

300m later fork L to much smaller FP along side of hill. FP continues through woods, reasonably level, climbing only gradually through pinewoods, and is clear and easy to follow apart from a short section across the top edge of a meadow after grass cutting. *(Note that red footprint waymarks are for raquettes de neige (snowshoe) routes.)*

At fork, 1–1.5km later, fork L downhill marked 'Dranse'. Continue ahead, up and down through woods, and 1km after that cross sturdy wooden FB over the river **Dranse**. Turn L on small FP on other side, which then becomes bigger, and 100m later reach junction with bend in gravel track. Here you have a choice (the first is shorter, the second avoids the main road).

OPTION A

The route to the L is marked 'Moulins'. Go downhill on gravel track, cross bridge over river and then follow the track steeply uphill between meadows to the main road some 50m before the **Chapelle Saint-Laurent** (1505) on the other side. *The building appears to be disused, but has a clear fresco of the Crucifixion scene outside above the doorway.* After this the waymarking stops, so turn R along the road (fields to either side) for 500m more to **Liddes**.

OPTION B

KSO(R) ahead on gravel track. Tarmac road joins from back R by farm (pilgrim sign) and KSO along it to junction by road bridge in

6km Dranse (925/20) 1250m
Restaurant.

Turn L, veering R on other side (resto to R at next hairpin bend). At junction at top turn L to road junction by two hotels/café/resto in

1km Liddes (926/19) Pop. 711, 1346m

Hôtel La Channe with café/resto and dormitory (027.783.14.15), Auberge des Alpes (027.783.13.80, info@auberge-des-alpes.ch), Hôtel Le Grand-Saint-Bernard, Rue du Fond de Ville 1 (027.783.13.02). Café de la Poste also has rooms. 2 small supermarkets, bank, TO.

Note The shop in Bourg Saint-Pierre (see below) has now closed, so make sure you stock up on any supplies you may need before you leave here; the next food shop isn't until Saint-Oyen – halfway down to Aosta on the Italian side!

Both routes Turn hard R at junction, up main street through village, past both shops, and KSO signed 'Bourg Saint Pierre 1h 40' and 'Palasui village'. At end, by church, cross main road and fork R downhill on other side, then fork L immediately onto upper of two tarmac tracks, with *barrage* (dam) below you to R and pass by **Palasui** village (1342m).

Track after Palasui

KSO, cross bridge over river, then tarmac becomes a gravel track. Then, when track bends L uphill, KSO ahead on walled lane with meadows (and Alpine flowers) to either side. When this bends hard L uphill (beehives) KSO ahead on grassy track on edge of wood, with river cascading down on your R and wall to L.

*Here you will find the first of a number of warnings about the dangers of going into river beds. These may look empty and innocent enough, but do **not** go down to them. Read (and heed) the many notices, in four languages, warning you that the water level can rise very suddenly and unexpectedly due to operations in the hydro-electric dams higher up (for example, when the floodgates are opened).*

200–300m later, at top of hill (**Allèves**, 1462m), cross sturdy wooden FB over (very fast-flowing) river. KSO(L) on other side on another walled lane between meadows. Main road above you is now much closer.

KSO(R) ahead at turning to L and continue uphill, gradually veering L to a minor road. Cross over and fork L uphill on other side (not clearly marked) up gravel track that takes you over the main road via the roof of its *galeria* (ie a 'lid' covering it to prevent it being blocked by snow) so that you then continue to LH side of main road, going down to meet it in a lay-by next to the bottom of a ski-lift. Fork L up small FP along its LH side, veering R before second pylon from top to reach gravel lane. Turn R and 100m later reach small **Chapelle de Notre-Dame de Lorette** (1663), perched on a rocky promontory overlooking the valley. *(The figure on a painting/altarpiece over the altar resembles a pilgrim.)*

Go downhill, continue parallel to road, then go under it and continue on other side past **Hôtel Bivuoac Napoléon**, leading down to main street. KSO(L) ahead here, go under main road and continue to church in

6km Bourg Saint-Pierre (932/13) 1632m

No shop. Maison Saint-Pierre, gîte d'étape with K in former priory stables, dating from 1726 (079.221.16.89, info@bivouac.ch). CH La Prieuré by church (027.783.17.23 or 079.637.39.44). Auberge du Petit-Vélan, with dormitory (027.787.11.41). Auberge Les Charmettes (X Wed, Thurs) with dormitory (027.787.11.50). Hôtel du Crêt, with dormitory (027.787.11.43). Hostellerie Le Moulin (027.787.11.69). Hôtel Bivouac Napoléon (027.787.11.62). Camping du Grand-Saint-Bernard (027.787.14.11 or 079.370.98.22).

Eglise Saint-Pierre (Mass on Sat evening, but no Sunday service), reconstructed on site of original 10th-century church, has very nice modern stained-glass windows including Saint Peter himself and three saints who were Swiss or were active in Switzerland – Saint-Maurice d'Agaune,

Looking down over Bourg Saint-Pierre

Saint-Nicholas de Fluë and Saint-Bernard d'Aoste (de Menton). References in pre-820 texts indicate that there was formerly a small monastery and hospice, 8th–9th centuries, in Bourg Saint-Pierre, thus preceding the one at the Great Saint Bernard Pass.

Stage XLIX (Petracastel, 49) in Sigeric's itinerary is the last on the journey through Switzerland for the modern pilgrim – though not for Sigeric, who was on his way back home to Canterbury. Stages XLVIII (Sce Remei, 48) and XLVII (Agusta, 47) are on the Italian side in, respectively, Saint-Rhémy-en-Bosses and Aosta.

At church fork R uphill on minor road, past lavoir, then at last house (bend) fork steeply L downhill on wide grassy track and cross a wooden bridge 500m later. Continue uphill on other side and then turn hard L uphill. KSO uphill, steeply, then down again, and reach a bridge and track arriving from the L, shortly before the dam wall. Zigzag steeply uphill on FP to reach the **Barrage de Toules** (1730m) and then, at the top, turn R on gravel track and go towards the waterworks building at side of dam (seat). KSO(L) at fork here (on the level for a short while).

When track does a very sharp bend hard R, KSO on FP ahead, turn L over wooden FB to cross river and KSO up steep rocky path on other side, veering R to become a better path leading to small abandoned farm building ahead. Continue downhill on grassy track, steep at first but then more gradual, that runs the length of the dam below you to L, then gradually uphill with river to your L instead. Pass small stone building ▼ closer to the Oleoduc sign 6 than 7 and KSO uphill.

In bad visibility turn L over FB and go to road instead. This is Bourg Saint-Bernard, where the tunnel under the Great St Bernard Pass starts – with its own road – so there will be less traffic than before on what has now become the old road over the Great St Bernard Pass.

When FP divides, KSO(R) uphill on narrow FP marked with yellow 'lozenges', up and over the shoulder of hill, then reach junction of paths by a concrete structure. Do **not** go down to the FB over to the L, but continue ahead on flank of hillside until you reach **La Pierre**, 2040m (an *alpage* – high mountain pasture used only in summer). Go through a small gate next to the building, leading to a bigger track, zigzagging to cross a bridge over the river. KSO, cross a second bridge, veering L towards the road, but shortly before you reach it turn R on grassy track, parallel to and beneath the road. 500m later reach the road at

11km L'Hospitalet (943/2) 2120m

As its name suggests, there was probably some kind of hospice/shelter for pilgrims and other travellers here in the past, but today there is just a round concrete structure – a 'chimney' (ventilation shaft for the road tunnel below) – by the side of the road at a bend (but offering shade/protection from the rain).

From time to time you will see information boards at the side of the road with Napoleon's hat, explaining the journey he made over the Alps on 20 May 1800, accompanied by 46,292 soldiers...

Note If you find quite a lot of deep snow up here, which is possible even in summer, you will have to continue on the road, 4km to the col.

Cross the road and continue on FP on other side. Reach road again shortly afterwards at hairpin bend, where the FP goes round it before veering R uphill steeply to the brow of a hill by an HT pylon, levelling out for a while after that, above the road below you to your R. KSO ahead at hairpin bend. Small FP but well waymarked with yellow 'lozenges'.

KSO along hillside then veer L to cross FB. Continue veering L uphill, stepped in places, but then it levels out. 1km later pass **Les Tronches**, 2270m, near a bend in the road, with a stone hut and another ventilation shaft. KSO on the RH of two paths, more steps visible ahead, veering R to wide stone track. KSO uphill.

As you round a bend you will see first a small cross on the skyline above you, and then the café at the pass and hospice come into view. The last 300m rise steeply uphill up the Combe des Morts, an old cobbled track ending up on a rough path and emerging, at 8114ft above sea level, at the

2km Col du Grand Saint-Bernard (945/0) 2473m

Slightly more than the halfway point on your journey to Rome. It is likely to be very cold here at night, even in mid-summer. The road route up to the pass is open only between late May/early June and mid-October (during which period there is a bus service three times a day from Martigny down to Aosta and back), so at other times the only way to get up (or down) from here – to either Bourg Saint-Pierre on the Swiss side or Saint-Rhémy-les-Bosses in Italy, after which you can take the bus which goes through the tunnel under the col – is on skis or with raquettes (snowshoes).

The Hospice du Grand-Saint-Bernard was founded by Saint-Bernard d'Aoste (Saint-Bernard de Menton) in 1050 to accommodate pilgrims and other travellers and has been in continuous use for nearly 1000 years. It has never closed in all that time, unlike most other hospices which, although they still exist, have had interruptions in their activity. Today it is run by the *chanoines reguliers* (not monks, but priests active in the surrounding community) who follow the rule of Saint Augustine, plus a relay of lay volunteer help in the summer months, and has dormitory-style accommodation plus some single and double rooms for walkers, pilgrims and others who want to spend a few quiet days there. Mass Sat 8.30pm, Sun 10.30am. Monastic offices daily (held in crypt chapel) – *liturgie* and *lecture, laudes, prière du midi, vêpres, complies*. The hospice also has a small treasury and offers video presentations (in French, German, Italian and English) about its history and work.

Hôtel de l'Hospice is owned and run by the Hospice, who opened it in the early 20th century to deal with the increasing numbers of travellers whom they were unable to accommodate in the hospice itself. (Cheaper rates during the week than at weekends, 027.787.11.53, ch.carrupt@ bluewin.ch). Café/resto Montjoux. Hotel Italia on Italian side of border.

The Musée/*chenil* (kennel) gives the history of the Saint Bernard dogs, but these are no longer used for rescue purposes; despite being very strong they are not only extremely heavy – to transport in a helicopter, for example – but difficult to train, so today German Shepherds are used instead; they are much lighter, so that two can be taken (in a helicopter) at a time if needed,

Mortuary at Col du Grand Saint-Bernard

and are easily trained. However, Saint Bernard dogs are still bred (and one or two of them trained for avalanche rescue) and live in the chenil in the summer (in the winter they are taken down to Martigny), where you can see them either resting in their very large cages or being taken for long walks each day in the surrounding area. Visitors can also accompany them on their daily walks (two levels – both 'sportif' and shorter/slower – ask in the TO if you are interested).

Whether you are walking on to Rome or stopping here, a two-night stay is recommended both to rest up and to collect your thoughts a little before either returning home or continuing on through Italy to complete your pilgrimage.

To continue, go under the bridge linking the hospice to the hotel and 100m later, halfway along the lakeside, cross the border into **ITALY**.

To return home If you want to break your journey here, but would find it easier to return home from the Italian side, you can either take the bus (mid-June to mid-September) down to Aosta (580m), journey time 1hr, or walk (28km), taking either one or two days (the route is well waymarked). From Aosta you can take

Exercising the Saint Bernard puppies

the train to Turin (and then on elsewhere) or the 'Pullman' (long-distance coach) to Milan.

Otherwise (to fly home from Geneva, for example) you can take the bus down to Orsières, the train from there to Martigny (changing in Sembrancher, but all is co-ordinated), and from there another train direct to the airport, total journey time about 3½hrs.

APPENDIX A
Further reading

General
Atwood, Donald and John, CR
Penguin Dictionary of Saints, 3rd edn
(Harmondsworth: Penguin, 1995)

Birch, Debra J
Pilgrimage to Rome in the Middle Ages (Studies in the History of Medieval Religion, vol. XIII)
(Woodbridge, Suffolk: Boydell Press, 1998)
A study of pilgrimage to Rome from Late Antiquity to the end of the 13th century, analysing motivation, routes and itineraries, different aspects of the journey such as travel and the dangers inherent in it, accommodation, special privileges granted to pilgrims, letters of recommendation, equipment, the blessing of scrip and staff, safe conduct, hospitality, exemption from tolls and notes on practical matters such as cost, when to go, etc.

Coleman, Simon and Elsner, John
Pilgrimage Past and Present in the World's Religions
(London: British Museum Press, 1995)

Davies, JG
Pilgrimage Yesterday and Today: why? where? how?
(London: SCM Press, 1988)
Studies the nature of pilgrimages and motives behind them, from patristic times to the Middle Ages, Protestant condemnation of pilgrimages and the 19th-century revival of pilgrimages amongst Protestants, ending with a review of the devotional aspects of modern pilgrmages.

Frey, Nancy Louise
Pilgrim Stories
(Berkley & Los Angeles: University of California Press, 1998)
This refers specifically to the experiences of modern pilgrims along the road to Santiago de Compostela, before, during and after making their pilgrimage, but the questions raised confront any modern pilgrim on a route where the journey itself, rather than the destination, is the real issue at stake.

Robinson, Martin
Sacred Places, Pilgrim Paths: an anthology of pilgrimage
(London: Fount, 1997)
An anthology reflecting the experiences of pilgrims through the ages, dealing with places of pilgrimage, preparation for the journey, the journey itself, the inner journey, worship on the way and on arrival, and the questions raised once the pilgrimage is over.

Spencer, Brian
Pilgrim Souvenirs and Secular Badges (Medieval finds from excavations in London)
(London: Stationery Office Books, 1998)
A study, by the former Keeper of the Museum of London, of pilgrim souvenirs and secular badges.

Sumption, Jonathan
Pilgrimage
(London: Faber and Faber, 1975)
A study of the traditions of pilgrimage prevalent in Europe from the beginnings of Christianity to the end of the 15th century, examining major destinations, motivations, the cult of the saints and their relics, medicine and the quest for cures, penitential pilgrimage, the practicalities of the journey and the pilgrims themselves.

Eade, John and Sallnow, Michael J (eds)
Contesting the Sacred: the anthropology of Christian pilgrimage
(London: Routledge, 1991)
Contributors examine particular Christian shrines (in France, Italy, Israel, Sri Lanka and Peru), analysing the dynamics of religious expression and belief, but also the political and economic processes at local and global levels, emphasising that pilgrimage is primarily an arena for competing religious and secular discourses.

French, RM (trans)
The Way of a Pilgrim
(London: Triangle, 1995)
First published in English in 1930 this book was written by an unknown Russian pilgrim in the 19th century, telling the story of his wanderings from one holy place to another in Russia and Siberia in search of the way of prayer.

Via Francigena
Chinn, Paul and Gallard, Babette
Walkers', Cyclists' and Horse Riders' Lightfoot Guide to the Via Francigena
(Arles: EURL Pilgrimage Publications, 2004)
A three-volume route-finding guidebook, mainly for cyclists, to the Via Francigena from Canterbury to Rome, with a fourth volume covering the cultural and historical aspects of this route.

Grégoire, Jean-Yves
La Via Francigena. Sur la trace des pèlerins de Canterbury à Rome
(Editions Ouest-France, 2010)
A concise introduction to the history and route of the Via Francigena, accompanied by numerous photos.

Magoun, Francis P, Jr
'An English pilgrim-diary of the year 990', in *Medieval Studies*, 2 (1940), pp. 231-52
Examination of the pilgrim-diary associated with Sigeric, Archbishop of Canterbury, from 990–94, and describing the route he took on his return journey.

Magoun, Francis P, Jr
'The Rome of two northern pilgrims: Archbishop Sigeric of Canterbury and Abbot Nikolas of Munkatheverà', in *Harvard Theological Review*, 33 (1940), pp. 267–89

Marques, William
'Why throw your badge away?', in *CPR Newsletter*, 1 (June 2007), pp. 6–11
Discusses the history of pilgrim badges in Britain, with particular reference to those from Rome.

Ortenberg, Veronica
'Archbishop Sigeric's journey to Rome in 990', in *Anglo-Saxon England*, 19, pp. 197–246
Identification of the places Sigeric stayed in on his return journey.

Quaglia, L
La Maison du Grand-Saint-Bernard des origines aux temps actuels
(Aosta 1955 and subsequent editions)

Robins, Peter
'Meaning and Usage of the Word "Francigena"', in *CPR Newsletter* 9 (April 2010), pp. 2–9

Zweidler, Reinhard
Der Frankenweg – Via Francigena. Der mittelalterliche Pilgerweg von Canterbury nach Rom
(Stuttgart: Konrad Theiss Verlag, 2003)
Discusses the history of the Via Francigena, from Canterbury all the way to Rome, and everyday pilgrim life in the Middle Ages, and describes the places along the way – geography, scenery, art and architecture.

Personal accounts
Belloc, Hilaire
The Path to Rome
(London: Allen & Unwin, 1955)
An account of the author's journey on foot from eastern France to Rome.

Browne, Peter Francis
Rambling on the Road to Rome
(London: Hamish Hamilton, 1990)
An account of the author's journey along the road to Rome taken by Hilaire Belloc – travelogue rather than pilgrimage.

Brunning, Anthony
'Pilgrim to Rome', in *CPR Newsletter* 2 (December 2007), pp. 2–23
An account of the author's walking pilgrimage from Canterbury to Rome in 1990.

Donaldson, Christopher
In the Footsteps of St Augustine. The Great English Pilgrimage from Rome to Canterbury
(Norwich: The Canterbury Press, 1995)
Re-creation of the journey from Rome to Canterbury made by Saint Augustine and his 40 companions in the year 597, sent by Pope Gregory the Great to bring Christianity to Britain. Part personal diary of the author's own journey along this route, the book is useful for the historical background to this event and as a guide for the future pilgrim to the 'sights' of Early Christian Rome.

Hughes, Gerard
In Search of a Way. Two Journeys of Spiritual Discovery
(London: Darton, Longman and Todd, 2nd edn 1986)
An account of a walking pilgrimage from Weybridge to Rome in 1975, with reflections on two journeys, the first made to find direction in the second. The

physical travel, on foot, lasted ten weeks, but the accompanying spiritual journey still continues.

Lambert, Christopher
Taking a Line for a Walk – 1000 Miles on Foot from Le Havre to Rome
(Woodbridge, Suffolk: Antique Collectors' Club Ltd, 2004)
A colour facsimile of the author's journal when he walked from Le Havre to Rome in 2000, via Lausanne and the Via Francigena. This book reproduces, on a double-page spread for each day, his handwritten text and several hundred colour-wash pen and ink drawings.

Other
Geoffrey Chaucer, trans. Coghill, Neville
The Canterbury Tales
(London: Penguin Classics, 1977)

Via Francigena
Twice-yearly magazine (Italian and English) published by Associazione Europea dei Comuni sulla Via Francigena, www.revistafrancigena.it

APPENDIX B
Useful contacts

Confraternity of Pilgrims to Rome
Tel: +44 7739 647426
www.pilgrimstorome.org.uk
pilgrimstoromesecretary@yahoo.com

Stanfords
12 Long Acre
Covent Garden
London WC2E 9LP
Tel: 020 7836 1321
www.stanfords.co.uk

The Map Shop
15 High Street
Upton-upon-Severn
Worcs WR8 0HJ
Tel: 01684 593146
www.themapshop.co.uk

FUAJ (Fédération Unie des Auberges de Jeunesse)
27 Rue Payol, 75018 Paris
Tel: 01.44.89.87.27
fuaj@fuaj.org

LFAJ (Ligue Française pour les Auberges de Jeunesse)
67 Rue Vergniand, Bâtiment K
75013 Paris
Tel: 01.44.16.75.78
info@auberges-de-jeunesse.com

Schweizer Jugendherbergen
Schaffhauserstrasse 14
CH-8042 Zürich
044.360.14.14
contact@youthhostel.ch

APPENDIX C
Index of maps

APPENDIX D
Index of principal place names

APPENDIX E
Summary of route

Principal place names are in **bold**.

NOTES

LISTING OF CICERONE GUIDES

For full information on all our guides, and to order books and eBooks, visit our website: **www.cicerone.co.uk**.

Walking – Trekking – Mountaineering – Climbing – Cycling

Over 40 years, Cicerone have built up an outstanding collection of 300 guides, inspiring all sorts of amazing adventures.

Every guide comes from extensive exploration and research by our expert authors, all with a passion for their subjects. They are frequently praised, endorsed and used by clubs, instructors and outdoor organisations.

All our titles can now be bought as **e-books** and many as iPad and Kindle files and we will continue to make all our guides available for these and many other devices.

Our website shows any **new information** we've received since a book was published. Please do let us know if you find anything has changed, so that we can pass on the latest details. On our **website** you'll also find some great ideas and lots of information, including sample chapters, contents lists, reviews, articles and a photo gallery.

It's easy to keep in touch with what's going on at Cicerone, by getting our monthly **free e-newsletter**, which is full of offers, competitions, up-to-date information and topical articles. You can subscribe on our home page and also follow us on **Facebook** and **Twitter**, as well as our **blog**.

Cicerone – the very best guides for exploring the world.

CICERONE

2 Police Square Milnthorpe Cumbria LA7 7PY
Tel: 015395 62069 info@cicerone.co.uk
www.cicerone.co.uk